CHALLENGES TO INDIAN FISCAL FEDERALISM

T.M. THOMAS ISAAC is the Minister of Finance of Kerala, an office he previously served from 2006 to 2011. Author of numerous academic papers and books, he was Professor at the Centre for Development Studies, Thiruvananthapuram. During his tenure as a member of the Kerala State Planning Board, he was in charge of the People's Plan Campaign, a landmark in decentralized planning. He is the author, with Michelle Williams, of *Building Alternatives: The Story of India's Oldest Construction Workers' Cooperative* (LeftWord 2017), and with Richard W. Franke, of *Local Democracy and Development: People's Campaign for Decentralised Planning in Kerala* (LeftWord 2000).

R. MOHAN took voluntary retirement from his position as Commissioner of Income Tax (Appeals) in 2016. He is currently a Senior Consultant in Gulati Institute of Finance and Taxation (GIFT) and Visiting Fellow, Centre for Development Studies (CDS). He is a member of Kerala Public Expenditure Review Committee. He is the author of several research papers.

LEKHA CHAKRABORTY is Associate Professor, National Institute of Public Finance and Policy, New Delhi, and Research Scholar, The Levy Economics Institute of Bard College, New York (NY), USA. She is the author of *Fiscal Consolidation, Budget Deficit and Macroeconomic Activity: Monetary Fiscal Policy Linkages* (New Delhi 2016).

CHALLENGES TO INDIAN FISCAL FEDERALISM

T.M. Thomas Isaac

R. Mohan

Lekha Chakraborty

LeftWord

First published in January 2019.
Reprinted November 2019.

LeftWord Books
2254/2A Shadi Khampur
New Ranjit Nagar
New Delhi 110008
INDIA

LeftWord Books and Vaam Prakashan are the publishing division of Naya Rasta Publishers Pvt. Ltd.

leftword.com

ISBN 978-81-934666-0-5

Dedicated to the memory of

Dr. Ashok Mitra

and

Prof. I.S. Gulati

whose studies and arguments in the cause of
a more balanced federal system have inspired us
and whose stance we try to emulate.

CONTENTS

TABLES AND FIGURES

TABLES

FIGURES

ACKNOWLEDGEMENTS

As persons engaged in academic, legislative and administrative aspects of public finance, the long run trends and the emerging scenario in Centre-State relations have always had a pride of place in our thinking. Issues in inter-governmental fiscal relations in India had earlier provoked many debates leading to the appointment of commissions and amendments to the Constitution. It is our considered opinion that at present, there is a sufficient vacant academic space for a discussion bringing to the fore the challenges facing Indian fiscal federalism. In attempting to fill this gap, we have tried our best to carry forward the scholarly traditions in the studies pioneered by Ashok Mitra, I.S. Gulati, K.K. George, B.P.R. Vithal and M.L. Sastry.

We owe much to the participants of the Southern Finance Ministers' conclave held in Thiruvananthapuram on 10th April, 2018, who gave meaningful inputs which we helped us to develop the theme of this book. In this context, special mention is due to C. Rammanohar Reddy, M. Govinda Rao, Sudipto Mundle and V. Bhaskar.

In this endeavour, we have received valuable help and cooperation from many of our colleagues and friends. We have immense gratitude to C.P. Chandrasekhar and Jayati Ghosh for their patience in going through the draft, offering valuable suggestions and writing the foreword. We express sincere thanks to V.G. Manamohan, S. Abhilash, R. Ajithkumar, T.C. Sethunath and S. Rananath of the office of Minister for Finance, Government of Kerala, for data support and secretarial assistance. V. Sriram, Librarian, Centre for Development Studies, Thiruvananthapuram, D. Shyjan, Head of the Department of Economics, University of Calicut, and V.K. Anil Kumar, Laurie Baker Centre for Habitat Studies, Thiruvananthapuram, tendered timely help in providing many relevant references, without which we would not have been able to complete this book in the short time frame.

C.P. CHANDRASEKHAR AND JAYATI GHOSH

FOREWORD

The framers of India's Constitution, faced with the vast size and immense diversity of the country, and conscious of the need to strengthen the national unity generated by the freedom movement, chose a complex, quasi-federal structure. While decentralization and devolution constituted one plank of the founding document, a strong national government was the other. Besides the specific framework of parliamentary democracy, involving elected representation to the State legislatures and the two houses of the national Parliament, the Constitution also allocated governance responsibilities between the Centre and the States. Where that was difficult to do, it took recourse to a Concurrent List of powers, responsibilities for which were ambiguously distributed.

The challenge did not end at that point. Both administration and development require finance, and in actual practice only a small proportion of tax revenues are collected by the State governments. The capacity to mobilize resources is much greater at the national level than at the level of individual States, as the latter are constrained by the level and structure of their incomes. The principle of subsidiarity requires lower levels of governments to undertake development activities which they can do better because of their being closer to the ground. This implies that the spending responsibilities of the States would require financing in excess of what they can effectively mobilize on their own. Further, differences in structural features and uneven development mean that there are substantial differences in the capacities of different States to garner resources, which in turn requires their redistribution. Vertical and horizontal inequities are, therefore, structurally embedded in the system and need to be addressed by combining both principles and flexibility.

To balance the multiple objectives of adequate devolution, addressing inter-State inequalities, and ensuring availability of resources for needed central expenditures, the Constitution provided for a Finance Commission instituted once in every five years to determine the share of resources to be devolved to the States and the principles that should govern the sharing of devolved resources between the States. However, this was not the only route through which resources were transferred to the States. A second channel was support provided to the State plans and for central projects implemented in the States through the Planning Commission, which was not a constitutionally created body, but functioned through discussion with the States. In addition, resources flowed through channels like the Development Finance institutions, which were provided financial support by the Reserve Bank of India and through the central budget. Clear principles of devolution or discussion with the States were largely absent in the case of these latter flows. Thus, in practice, an imperfect multi-channel system for resource flows was created through conscious design, and this needed to be revisited periodically to ensure the fairness that was crucial for strengthening the unity of a socially and economically diverse nation.

An abiding problem has been that, despite the efforts of the founding fathers of the Indian Constitution, the scope for discretion was substantial in the structure determining the sharing of resources between the Centre and the States and among the States. So, commitment to principles, and democratic scrutiny and accountability were needed to ensure that the system served its multiple objectives as best as possible. Needless to say, the actual devolution of resources as it evolved in practice has been controversial right from the start, mainly because of the perception that the Centre has retained for itself a disproportionate share of resources and influenced (for political reasons) the distribution of resources between the States. In addition, some States have felt that they have been unfairly treated in the sharing of devolved resources.

This deviation of results from the intent of the framers of the Constitution has only widened during the years of neoliberal reforms. Committed to incentivizing private business with a lenient tax regime, the Centre reneged on its responsibility to enhance resource mobilization through taxation substantially. To retain for itself a larger share of the taxes actually mobilized, it resorted to devices like imposing cesses that did not fall within the remit of the revenue-sharing decisions of the Finance Commissions. Wanting to ensure its presence in the limited development activities being pursued in the States, it also sought to centralize more of these in the form of centrally sponsored schemes, an increasing share of the costs of which the States were called upon to bear. At the Centre's urging, the distribution of plan funds and grants-in-aid through the Planning Commission became more political and controversial. And, finally, and most importantly, the Finance Commissions, constitutionally mandated to be independent bodies concerned principally with fair revenue sharing, were sought to be made the instruments of central policy through manipulation of membership and the Terms of Reference, especially starting with the 11th Finance Commission. This was reflected not only in decisions on revenue sharing, but in the imposition of conditions on State governments. The consequence of this is the erosion of the already limited fiscal autonomy of the States. They were also forced to adopt policies in keeping with the Centre's neoliberal shift, even when they were inclined otherwise. Nothing reflected the success of this project more than the adoption of Fiscal Responsibility and Budget Management Acts by most State governments. There were exceptions such as the 14th Finance Commission, that appeared to be more even-handed in its revenue sharing recommendations. But at present, an effort to revise even those marginal improvements is already underway.

Much has been written about these trends and the damaging impact that they have had on the fiscal and policy autonomy of the States. Yet, this contribution from Thomas Isaac and his co-authors is a key addition to this literature for at least four reasons. First, Isaac as economist, columnist, four-time member of the Legislative Assembly, and most importantly Finance Minister of the State of Kerala for one full term and a second currently underway, has had an insider view and been at the centre of debates on the evolution of Centre–State relations for more than two decades. Second, in this book they take the debate forward by capturing the implications of the abolition of the Planning Commission, the introduction of the controversial Goods and Services Tax regime, and formulation of Terms of Reference of the recently constituted 15th Finance Commission. These include the increase in vertical fiscal inequity, distortion of fairness in inter-State distribution (through the specification of 2011 as the reference year for population estimates), and erosion of policy autonomy at the level of the States. Third, Isaac, the first author, has been in the unusual position of being in the leadership of the unique effort by the State of Kerala to advance the devolution process beyond that from the Centre to the States, to that from the State level to the panchayats and municipalities. Besides taking the path-breaking decision to devolve 40 per cent of State plan funds to local government institutions, the Kerala experiment involved a mass campaign to build capacity of local government and involve local expertise in the effort to use those funds. Isaac and his co-authors' argument, therefore, is that protecting and enhancing devolution is also required for strengthening popular participation in development decision-making. And, finally, this book is being published at a time when some of the State finance ministers have been leading a campaign on the need for revisiting certain Terms of Reference of the 15th Finance Commission. This involvement in a movement to reverse the tendency to erode both the fiscal and policy autonomy of the State by misusing a statutory institution that does not have the constitutional mandate to interfere in many matters that the ToR of the 15th FC refers to, gives the book an edge and urgency that is likely to place it at the centre of the debate on the attack on Indian federalism.

The authors deploy this rare combination of characteristics and experience to address an intensely contested and topical issue. This delivers an engaging book that is at once informative, educative and inspiring. Hopefully, it would also influence thinking on an issue that is central to the health of India's democratic polity.

CHAPTER 1

INDIAN FEDERALISM: MAJOR CHALLENGES

Federalism is an inalienable part of the basic structure of the Indian Constitution. As adumbrated by the Supreme Court in the Keshavananda Bharati case, the basic structure of the Constitution is beyond the pale of amendment by a Parliamentary majority. But, we fear that this is precisely what is being attempted in the fiscal realm through overt and covert actions of the central government. It is this challenge that this book seeks to address. Though we shall present the broad trends since Independence in Centre–State financial relations, our focus is on the developments during the last two decades, and particularly since the notification of the Terms of Reference (ToR) of the 15th Finance Commission. As the Memorandum submitted by the group of State Finance Ministers to the President of India warned, they would 'impact not only the finances of the State governments but also undermine the fabric of our federal polity' (Finance Ministers 2018).

SIGNIFICANCE AND RATIONALE OF FISCAL FEDERALISM

The significance of federalism for the unity and development of our country cannot be understated. In a country vast in terms of geography and population, like India, it is important to have a governance structure that would protect the needs and aspirations of the regions without sacrificing the larger common good of the nation.

Our nation evolved through the anti-imperialist struggle against British rule. The cardinal principle of the freedom movement was unity in diversity. The language-based regional Pradesh Congress Committees were a recognition of this ideal. Without encouraging the full cultural and social development of the sub-national regions, it is not possible to ensure the unity of the country.

QUASI FEDERALISM?

Surprisingly, when the Constitution was framed, several unitary features found a pride of place in it. It is for this reason that many have chosen to describe India as quasi-federal. The broad colonial legal structure of the Montague–Chelmsford Reforms (1919) and Government of India Act (1935), was carried over into the Indian Constitution (Gulati and George 1988).

As E.M.S. Namboodiripad (1968) commented, the Constitution was drawn up in the emotional context of India's Partition. As a consequence, the emphasis was more on the unity of the country rather than the autonomy of the States. Initially, the Constitution did not even accept the principle of language-based States. It was only after the mass agitations in Andhra and Maharashtra that the principle of linguistic States was adopted.

In the legislative sphere, though there are distinct Union and State Lists (Seventh Schedule of the Constitution), there is also a Concurrent List, where the central government has overriding powers. Besides, the Residuary powers are also vested with the Centre. The Centre has the discretion to legislate on subjects in the State List (Article 249) and give directions to the States (Articles 256, 257 and 355). The Centre does not have the need to consult States in entering into international treaties, even when they have a key bearing on the subjects falling in the State List[1] (Noorani 2012).

[1] The ASEAN Treaty which provides for lowering import duty on commodities like natural rubber has been entered into without consulting the States

On the whole, reviewing the trends during the last seven decades, there is evidence of a steady encroachment into the legislative spheres of the States mainly through enlarging the Concurrent List and also through entering into international treaties as part of the globalization process, in the recent years.

In the sphere of administration, the right of the central government to intervene in the States is nearly unconditional and open. Articles 256 and 257 give wide powers to the central government to issue directions to the State administration. The much-abused Article 356 gives power to the central government to dismiss elected State governments, if it perceives a 'constitutional breakdown' in the State. The Governor, the formal head of the State administration, is appointed by the central government and in a substantial number of instances, without consulting the State governments and on purely partisan considerations (see Austin 1966, Shah 2017, for a detailed discussion).[2] The most recent case has been the blatant misuse of the office of the Lt Governor in Delhi,[3] where the formal head claimed to have overriding powers over elected ministry, finally compelling the Supreme Court to intervene. In fact, the only silver lining in an ever darkening horizon has been the 1993 Supreme Court judgement in the S.R. Bommai case, where certain restrictions were placed on imposition and continuance of President's rule in the States. Despite, the

concerned which will have to address the issue of affected farmers whose welfare is a State subject.

[2] These issues were raised by the Rajamannar Committee Report (1971) and Memorandum submitted by the Left Front government of West Bengal in 1977. These two suggested substantial political and fiscal devolution of power to the States.

[3] See judgement of the Supreme Court in *Government of NCT of Delhi vs Union of India & Another,* Civil Appeal No. 2357 of 2017, in which the Chief Justice of India observed, 'If a well deliberated legitimate decision of the Council of Ministers is not given effect to due to an attitude to differ on the part of the Lieutenant Governor, then the concept of collective responsibility would stand negated.'

recommendations of the Sarkaria and M.M. Punchi Commissions on Centre–State relations (which submitted reports in 1987 and 2010 respectively) and Supreme Court judgements, even in recent times, we are not short of instances of dismissal of State governments and the manipulative use of the Governor's office for manufacturing a legislative majority.

In the financial sphere, as in most federations, in India also there is a serious mismatch between the functions and finances of the Union and that of the federating States. In India, the States spend around 60 per cent of the combined government expenditure, but collect only around 40 per cent of the combined revenues. Therefore, there is need for a constitutional mechanism to transfer resources to the States. The constitutional provision for the quinquennial appointment of an independent Finance Commission (hereafter FC), with a quasi-judicial character has this aim. There is also the objective of limiting the discretion of the Centre in the matter of resource flows to the States. The FCs determine the proportion of the taxes to be devolved to the States and also the principles of its distribution among the States. Tax devolution constitutes around 90 per cent of the total award of the FCs. The rest consists of special grants to the States facing revenue deficits even after tax devolution, minor specific-purpose grants, disaster management and grants for local governments since the 10th FC.

Besides, the FC channel, the Planning Commission[4] formed through an Executive Order in 1951, became an important source of fund flow to the States, partly through formula-based grants[5] and the balance through discretionary grants. This led to constraining the role of the FCs since the 1960s, to examine and make recommendations only on the non-plan revenue component of the State budgets, resulting in unwarranted segmentation in the disbursement of grants. Soon, a third channel of resource transfer,

[4] Now no longer in existence since the formation of NITI Aayog.

[5] A part of the plan grants was transferred through the Gadgil formula.

namely, Centrally Sponsored Schemes (CSS), which are included in the central plan, also became an important source of grants to the States, especially, since the 1970s. But these were tied flows for schemes whose criteria were rigidly fixed by the Centre, with the States being forced to share (an increasing) part of the cost of their implementation. This implied substantial central incursion into the subjects in the State List.

In addition to the above three, the Centre also gave discretionary grants to the States, after considering special needs. These grants, like the non-FC grants mentioned above were disbursed invoking provisions of Article 282 of the Constitution, which is classified under 'Miscellaneous Financial Provisions' meant to be used sparingly under special circumstances. But this constitutional provision has become the basis for routine disbursal of grants by the Centre to the States.

The multiplicity of sources of funds flow from the Centre to the States, not only distorted the constitutional intention of non-discretionary transfers but also stymied the expenditure priorities of the States, thus effectively undermining the fundamental principles of fiscal federalism sought to be constitutionally protected through the FCs. As a consequence, the contribution of FC awards in the total resource transfer to the States has tended to come down to less than 60 per cent until the 14th FC increased the share of taxes.

In the aftermath of economic liberalization, the role of the FCs itself underwent substantial changes. They became vehicles for enforcing and incentivizing fiscal reforms aimed at realizing deficit targets at the State level. This tendency has been visible since the 11th FC, with efforts to link disbursement of statutory grants and debt relief packages to the passing and implementation of Fiscal Responsibility and Budget Management (FRBM) Acts by the States. As a consequence States have been subjected to double jeopardy in recent years. Not only has the share of grants disbursed by the FCs fallen relative to other grants, but also the FCs have themselves started adopting roles not mandated by the Constitution, thereby adversely affecting the States.

The trends discussed above have had serious implications for State finances. The constraints imposed by the FCs since the 11th among them, have compelled the States to adhere to deficit targets lest they should lose the benefits made conditional on the realization of those targets. Though many States began recording revenue surpluses, there has been inefficiency in the management of borrowed funds. This problem worsened as the States chose not to spend for fear of breaching deficit targets set by the FCs as conditions for debt relief and rescheduling.

Further, in the globalization era, central taxes have not been very buoyant due to the many tax concessions given and rate reductions implemented to incentivize the private sector. The divisible pool of taxes also shrank as a consequence. The increasing reliance on surcharges and cesses, revenues from which are not shareable with the States, and their rising share in gross tax revenue, is another reason for this. These along with an inherent bias in setting rates of Goods and Services Taxes (GST) and apportioning revenues from them between the Centre and the States, have worsened the vertical fiscal imbalances between the Centre and the States. This has happened despite increased devolution of shareable taxes from the Centre to the States by the 14th FC.

CHAPTER SCHEME

As stated earlier, the intent of this book is to examine in detail the implications of three important policy changes connected with economic reforms, namely, the FRBM Acts, the GST scheme and the Terms of Reference of the 15th FC on Centre–State financial relations. The chapter-wise content and intent are summarized below.

Chapter 2. Union and State Finances: Emerging Issues

We intend to preface our analysis with a brief review of the trends in Centre–State finances in the post-Independence period in Chapter 2.

The most important feature of Indian public finance has been the rapid rise in the expenditure of the governments, both at the central and State levels, when compared with the colonial period. While during the colonial period the government broadly adopted a laissez-faire policy and kept all-government expenditure at less than 10 per cent, independent India chose a path of planned development of a market economy with a significant public sector presence, which could not have been undertaken without a sharp increase in government expenditure. Indeed, the ratio of government expenditure to Gross Domestic Product (GDP) crossed 25 per cent in the mid-1980s. Since then, it has fluctuated around this figure within a band of 3-4 percentage points. How was this expenditure financed? What was the contribution of tax and non-tax revenues of the States and Centre? What was the trend in central transfers to the States? In the absence of sufficient buoyancy of tax revenues, what were the trends in fiscal and revenue deficits? A discussion of these questions leads us to an analysis of the fiscal crisis of the Indian state.

Chapter 3. Worsening Vertical Fiscal Imbalance

The States in India also contributed to the rising trend in government spending and, therefore, they also emerged as key players in the development process. It may also be noted that there have been substantial differences in the regional pattern of development. There have been States like those in western India that exhibited very rapid industrial development, but did not record remarkable achievements in education, health care and social welfare. In contrast, there have been States like Kerala which have been recognized for their social sector achievements, but performed relatively poorly in industrial development. Yet another category would be the States in the Gangetic plain that did not make significant advances in either industry or welfare. Of course, there can be no disagreement that what we require is a model with growth and equity. We have touched upon the comparative experience in regional development not to pass any judgement on any particular course, but to draw attention to the possibilities for the autonomy that existed at the level of the States and the dynamic role a State government could play within the quasi-federal system. It is in the context of this active role played by the State governments in the development process, that we discuss in this chapter the trend in vertical fiscal imbalance, i.e. the difference between overall expenditure of the States and their revenues, pre- and post-devolution. Given the rising fiscal responsibilities of the State governments, the extent of imbalances would depend upon the buoyancy of central revenues, the awards of the FC, and the success of the efforts of the central government to shrink the divisible pool of taxes by relying more on surcharges and cesses rather than on raising basic rates to mobilize resources and manipulate estimates of net proceeds of taxes collected by the Centre.

Chapter 4. Fiscal Responsibility and Budget Management Act: Its Impact on Fiscal Space

How are the key fiscal measures adopted consequent to FRBM Acts affecting the Centre–State fiscal imbalance that was outlined in the previous two chapters? This is taken up in Chapter 4, which examines the conceptual basis and implementation of the FRBM Acts at the central and State levels. The chapter provides both a theoretical critique of the FRBM Acts and a review of their implementation. We compare the performance of the FRBM Acts before and after the global economic crisis in 2008-09, which further reinforces the argument that there is nothing theoretically sacrosanct about any particular absolute level of the deficit or its size relative to domestic product. The Chapter also examines the relative success of fiscal consolidation at the central and the State levels. The States have little scope for deviation from FRBM targets and therefore there is an asymmetry in the burden imposed by the fiscal adjustment process on the Centre and the States. How this adversely impacts the fiscal manoeuvrability and autonomy in spending of the States is a vital issue. This is explored by examining the phenomenon of increase in unspent borrowed funds by the States.

Chapter 5. Post-GST Scenario: State Revenues Straitjacketed

Having examined the expenditure constraints imposed on the State governments, the discussion moves on to the constraints on the revenue side. Chapter 5 turns to a discussion of how the Goods and Services Tax is going to accentuate the vertical fiscal imbalances between the Centre and the States.

There are three factors to be considered, viz. 1) the rate apportionment between the Centre and the States; 2) the possibility of State governments tweaking the rates which existed even under the Value Added Tax (VAT) regime; and 3) the buoyancy of revenues under GST given the lackadaisical implementation. It is true that all States have been guaranteed a minimum increase in revenues of 14 per cent per annum from taxes subsumed under GST, but this is no consolation for the States faced with very high vertical fiscal imbalances that need to rapidly increase their revenues.

Though the introduction of the GST regime has been hailed by some as historic and a sign of the strength of India's 'cooperative' federalism, there is no denying the fact that it has resulted in the complete erosion of fiscal autonomy and loss of independent power to raise tax revenues at the State level. Moreover, we really do not see encouraging progress in terms of revenue buoyancy or economic growth since the introduction of the regime.

Chapter 6. Terms of References of 15th Finance Commission: Implications

The other important concern in the context of evolving inter-governmental fiscal relations in India is the linking of transfers to the States to their fiscal performance. It is true that the transfer system should not create perverse incentives. However, the spirit of fiscal federalism demands that transfers to the State cannot take the form of tied and conditional grants which distort the expenditure priorities of the States. Yet, the 11th FC, for the first time, was given a crucial mandate to take a holistic view of the finances of both the Centre and the States to suggest 'ways and means by which the governments, collectively and severally, may bring about a restructuring of the public finances so as to restore budgetary balance and maintain macroeconomic stability'. This was unwarranted since stabilization is a central government function and not that of the FC. Nevertheless, the 11th FC went on to recommend a plan of restructuring of public finances to improve the fiscal situation, involving setting of numerical targets for yearly reductions in revenue and fiscal deficits and conditionalities for releasing statutory grants under Article 275 of the Constitution to the States.

The 12th FC's restructuring plan also proposed numerical targets for deficit reduction, and went one step further by linking State-level debt relief and debt restructuring conditional upon the enactment of FRBM Acts. The 13th FC also prescribed time limits for achieving deficit targets. But the 14th FC changed the narrative by allowing States reaching deficit targets to have additional borrowing space.

There is high probability that the 15th FC would attempt to

build into its recommendations conditionalities favouring the suggestions made by the FRBM Review Committee. The committee has prescribed draconian targets such as a sharp reduction in the debt-to-GDP ratio to 60 per cent by 2022-23 from the present level of 68 per cent, and to achieve this, reducing the fiscal deficit of the Centre and States to 2.5 and 1.7 per cent respectively from the current equal rate of 3 per cent. Chapter 6 examines the implications of such a measure on the fiscal space of the States.

The ToR of the 15th FC explicitly mandates the commission to suggest conditionalities that might be imposed when permitting States to resort to public borrowing. It simultaneously speaks of elimination of revenue deficit grants to the States and also opens the door for a rollback of the 'enhanced devolution' awarded by the 14th FC, citing expenditure commitments of the Union. The calamitous impact of such measures on State finances is discussed, based on a detailed examination of the overall impact on resource transfers as a result of 14th FC award.

The undemocratic nature of some of the Terms of Reference, such as the one that seeks control of 'expenditure on populist measures', which tantamount to an incursion into the policy domain of democratically elected State governments is also underlined.

A mandate of that kind for a FC is both unprecedented and unwarranted. The bias inherent in these manoeuvres is clear from the fact that, while implementation of flagship welfare schemes of the Centre by the States is to be used as a performance indicator for becoming eligible for grants-in-aid, the welfare schemes of States are being dubbed as 'populist' and expenditure on them is sought to be controlled.

The ToR of the 15th FC, if not changed, have the potential to substantially alter the system of inter-governmental fiscal transfers. The consequence of this would be that the States would find it difficult to pursue independent fiscal initiatives in future, which would be contrary to their expected role in a robust federal system.

The basic constitutional principles in pursuit of which FCs were considered necessary have been diluted through inclusion of clauses like these in the ever expanding ToR of the FCs, with this trend scaling new heights in the ToR of the 15th FC. While it is a fact that our transfer system has several deficiencies, requiring correction, it should not be through heavy reliance on tied and conditional grants, but through an alternative, which accommodates and protects the objectives of equity, efficiency and autonomy of the States.

Chapter 7. Horizontal Fiscal Imbalances and Conflicting Interests of States

Chapter 7 analyses how far the FCs have been able to fulfil one of their main constitutional mandates of ensuring equalization of fiscal capacities across the States to the extent possible. The fiscal capacity of States in India varies widely and these differences have been increasing in the post-liberalization period. In this context FCs, as constitutional arbitrators, should not be burdened with ToR that restrict their corrective capacities. The proposed shifting in the reference population used from that in the 1971 census to that in the 2011 census is a case in point. That shift will adversely affect States that have successfully implemented the national population policy and will constitute a breach of the national commitment made when the policy was adopted. There have been strident objections to the move by the affected States, which are discussed in some detail in Chapter 7, which examines how equity concerns and efficiency considerations can be delicately balanced.

Chapter 8. Centre–State Relations and Empowering Local Governments

The 73rd and 74th Constitution amendments prescribe a uniform structure for local governments as a third tier of the federal system. True federalism requires decentralization that involves devolution of functions and funds from the Centre to the States and from the

States to the local governments. Unfortunately, many of the votaries of local governments have chosen to ignore the issue of Centre–State financial relations and view political decentralization to the third tier in isolation. Excepting for a few States, the devolution of functions, funds and functionaries from the State to local level have been meagre. Our analysis of the Union FC grants to the local governments assumes significance in this context.

Chapter 9. The Way Ahead:
Towards a Federal Democratic Polity

It is abundantly clear that with fiscally disempowered States, we cannot have a healthy and robust federal system. We need to ponder over effective alternatives in the light of rising vertical and horizontal imbalances in the fiscal realm. It is also essential to address the question of the feasibility of States pursuing region-specific and emulation-worthy development experiences, which had been a reality of the past. The question is to how to make the polity more democratic and ensure national progress for achievement of better human development. For this, the basic task is to transform cooperative federalism from a mere rhetoric, to one backed by measures which make it meaningful in practice.

CHAPTER 2

UNION AND STATE FINANCES: EMERGING ISSUES

The development strategy adopted at the time of Independence was premised on a growing and strategic role for government expenditure in it. The basic economic criticism of colonial rule made by the national movement was that it permitted unfettered imports that ruined domestic industries and adopted a laissez-faire attitude that impeded economic development. Therefore, the twin slogans of swadeshi and planned development were central to the national movement (see Chandra, Mukherjee and Mukherjee 2008 for a detailed discussion). The adoption of an import substitution-based development strategy and public sector-led five year development plans were the cardinal features of independent India's economic policy (Chakravarthy 1987, Patnaik 1979, Byres 1979). The success of that strategy depended on an expansion of the protected domestic market and on adequate mobilization of resources by the government. Here, we are concerned with the success and limitations of government resource mobilization to finance the inevitable expansion of expenditure within the prevailing frame of Centre–State financial relations.

In this chapter, we undertake a review of revenue, expenditure, deficit and debt trends of the Centre and the States, and analyse the long-run movement of major fiscal indicators. The time period of our analysis is 1970-71 to 2016-17. In the case of borrowing and other liabilities we have analysed data from 1980-81 to 2016-17. In the constitutional division of functions and finance, there is an inherent imbalance in the revenue raising power and expenditure responsibilities between the Union and States. We analyse the trends in this imbalance during the last five decades and examine the movements in deficits and debt over that time period here.

TRENDS IN RECEIPTS AND EXPENDITURE

In Table 2.1 (overleaf), we give a bird's eye view of the revenue receipts and total expenditure of the central and State governments. A comparable combined expenditure series is available only from 1980-81 (adjusted for the net lendings to the States by the Centre and the central grants). Nevertheless, we have included decadal first year figures for the earlier decades so as to provide a long-run perspective.

The most remarkable feature is the rapid growth in ratio of combined expenditure of the States and the Centre to GDP from 8.79 per cent of GDP in 1950-51 to 27.50 per cent in 2015-16, in contrast to the long-run stagnation at around 10 per cent of GDP during the colonial period (Kumar 1989). The rapid upward trend continued during the 1980s, with the figure reaching a peak of 28.27 per cent in 1986-87. Thereafter it declined and stagnated. The growth in expenditure was being constrained by limitations on resource mobilization. The combined revenue of the Centre and States rose from 7.56 per cent of GDP in 1950-51 to 18.04 during 1986-87 and thereafter stagnated around that level for the next two decades. As a result, the resource gap, i.e. the difference between combined expenditure and combined revenue receipts, that had increased from 1.23 per cent of GDP in 1950-51 reached 10.23 per cent during 1986-87 and hovered around 9 per cent until 1990-91

(Table 2.1). This resource gap had to be bridged by deficit financing with attendant inflationary consequences, given supply constraints. The key failure was in revenue resource mobilization which did not keep pace with expenditure. It may be noted that the revenue–GDP ratio of 18 per cent is much lower than the tax–GDP ratio of all the developed and middle-income countries, which is on an average above 25 per cent and in some cases above 40 per cent.[1] Suffice to say that the class limitations implicit in the development regime impeded mobilization of sufficient resources precisely from those classes that were the main beneficiaries of the development process.[2] As we shall see later, indirect taxes dominated as a share of revenues during this period.

The crisis resulting from the fiscal and current account deficits pushed the Indian economy onto the path of neoliberal reforms during the 1990s. The rising trend in the government expenditure to GDP ratio came to an end and it fluctuated around 25 per cent of GDP until the global financial crisis of 2008. Like most countries in the world, India also adopted an expansionary stimulus policy in response to the crisis as a result of which the expenditure to GDP ratio increased to 26-27 per cent in the subsequent years. As a consequence, the resource gap which had declined to below 5 per cent primarily because of a significant increase in the revenue to GDP ratio and mild downward trend in expenditure, rose once again to 9.80 per cent in 2009-10 and has been around 7 per cent thereafter. The expenditure compression during the 1990s was largely the result of the implementation of the FRBM Acts. The spike in the deficits in the post-global financial crisis period is

[1] See https://data.worldbank.org/indicator/GC.TAX.TOTL.GD.ZS for cross-country data on tax–GDP ratios.

[2] For an analysis of class relations and dominance, see Raj (1973), Namboodiripad (1973) and Bardhan (1984). The very narrow base of direct taxes and predominance of indirect taxes is a palpable indicator of this limitation.

Table 2.1: Revenues and expenditures of Centre and States (% of GDP)

Year	Revenues			Expenditures			Gap between combined and Expenditure and Revenues (7)=(4)–(1)
	Combined (1)	Centre (2)	States (3)	Combined (4)	Centre (5)	States (6)	
1950-51	7.56	4.67	2.90	8.79	4.90	4.55	1.23
1960-61	9.88	6.24	3.64	14.42	9.65	8.18	4.54
1970-71	12.31	7.99	4.31	16.93	9.92	9.12	4.62
1980-81	15.93	10.28	5.65	23.64	14.28	12.96	7.71
1981-82	16.43	10.53	5.90	23.06	13.54	12.40	6.63
1982-83	16.83	10.74	6.09	24.42	14.38	12.89	7.59
1983-84	16.14	10.35	5.79	24.32	14.52	12.83	8.18
1984-85	16.73	10.80	5.93	26.01	16.11	13.46	9.28
1985-86	17.62	11.63	5.99	26.39	17.41	13.72	8.77
1986-87	18.04	11.94	6.10	28.27	18.65	14.00	10.23
1987-88	18.15	11.81	6.34	27.63	17.74	14.44	9.48
1988-89	17.74	11.56	6.19	26.58	17.30	13.62	8.84
1989-90	18.39	12.13	6.25	27.03	17.80	13.68	8.64
1990-91	16.94	10.98	5.96	26.03	17.21	13.87	9.09
1991-92	18.05	11.38	6.67	25.49	16.01	14.38	7.44
1992-93	17.48	11.21	6.28	25.23	15.82	13.94	7.75
1993-94	16.52	9.92	6.59	24.96	15.90	13.70	8.44
1994-95	17.02	10.04	6.98	24.24	14.79	13.92	7.22
1995-96	16.89	10.29	6.60	23.44	14.20	13.35	6.55
1996-97	16.49	10.29	6.20	22.54	13.62	12.97	6.05
1997-98	16.41	10.63	5.77	23.39	13.21	13.32	6.98

1998-99	15.24	9.28	5.96	24.56	13.91	13.71	9.32
1999-00	16.17	9.85	6.32	25.40	14.30	14.47	9.23
2000-01	16.07	10.00	6.07	25.02	14.38	14.09	8.95
2001-02	16.10	9.63	6.47	25.67	14.71	14.48	9.57
2002-03	16.68	10.23	6.45	25.88	14.48	14.27	9.20
2003.04	17.48	10.68	6.80	26.25	12.66	15.13	8.77
2004-05	18.13	11.16	6.97	25.32	12.42	14.34	7.19
2005-06	18.85	11.67	7.18	25.16	13.45	14.14	6.31
2006-07	20.27	12.66	7.61	25.25	13.15	14.42	4.98
2007-08	20.20	13.55	6.65	24.85	14.08	13.34	4.65
2008-09	18.70	12.20	6.49	26.77	15.54	13.84	8.07
2009-10	18.15	11.16	6.99	27.95	15.64	14.76	9.80
2010-11	19.89	12.80	7.09	27.06	15.26	14.01	7.17
2011-12	18.32	11.11	7.22	26.06	14.28	13.98	7.74
2012-13	19.12	11.45	7.66	26.05	13.78	14.29	6.93
2013-14 (PE)	19.10	11.65	7.45	25.90	13.58	14.23	6.80
2014-15	20.76	11.68	9.08	27.99	13.40	17.39	7.23
2015-16 2nd RE	20.66	12.05	8.61	27.50	12.80	17.05	6.84

Source: *Indian Public Finance Statistics*, various years.

largely a reflection of the de facto pause in the pursuit of its FRBM targets by the central government.

The gap between revenues and expenditure necessitates borrowing by the government which runs up against the constraints set by the FRBM targets. The States, which are compelled to function within this framework through conditionalities imposed by the FCs are subject to an asymmetric burden vis-à-vis the Centre. To get a clearer picture of the issues, an examination of trends in receipts, expenditure and their components is very essential. We proceed to do that in the following sections of this chapter.

REVENUE RECEIPTS AND COMPONENTS: 1970-71 TO 2016-17

Tax Revenue

In the revenue receipts of the Centre and the States, a substantial part is revenue from taxes. Hence, the trends in tax revenue would throw more light on the resource mobilization efforts of the governments. The major sources of revenue for the central government are personal income tax, corporation tax on profits of companies, central excise duty on manufacturing, c duty on imports and service tax. Out of these, central excise (other than on petroleum products) and service tax have been subsumed in the GST since July 1, 2017. The share of indirect taxes in the Centre's gross tax revenue, which stood at 80 per cent during the 1980s, gradually came down to 49 per cent by 2016-17. But when the tax revenues of the Centre and the States are taken together, the share of indirect taxes is high even now. As far as the tax–GDP ratio of the Centre is concerned, the trend over the last four and a half decades shows only a marginal improvement, despite the economy growing much faster since the 1980s (Table 2.2).

The buoyancy of central taxes fell during the period 1970-71 to

Table 2.2: Decadal trends in own revenue and expenditure gap between Centre and the States, 1970-71 to 2016-17

Period	Ave. gross tax revenue–GDP ratio of the Centre (1)	Ave. own tax revenue–GDP ratio of all States (2)	Tax revenue gap (3)= (1)–(2)	Ave. revenue expenditure–GDP ratio of the Centre (4)	Ave. revenue expenditure–GDP ratio of all States (5)	Exp-enditure gap (6)= (4)–(5)
1970-71 to 1979-80	8.23	3.83	4.4	8.06	8.34	-0.28
1980-81 to 1989-90	9.54	4.91	4.63	11.05	11.06	-0.01
1990-91 to 1999-2000	8.99	5.04	3.95	11.89	12.17	-0.28
2000-01 to 2009-10	9.63	5.56	4.07	12.76	12.47	-0.29
2010–11 to 2016-17	10.36	6.24	4.19	12.24	12.75	-0.51
1970-71 to 2016-17	9.29	5.04	4.25	11.13	11.36	-0.23

Source: *Handbook of Statistics on Indian Economy*, RBI, various issues.

Table 2.3: Tax–GDP ratios and buoyancy estimates of Centre and States, 1970-71 to 2016-17

Period	Tax–GDP ratio (Centre & States)	Centre Tax–GDP ratio	States Tax–GDP ratio	Central Tax buoyancy	All-States Tax buoyancy
1970-71 to 1979-80	12.06	8.23	3.83	1.62	1.54
1980-81 to 1989-90	14.45	9.54	4.91	1.09	1.13
1990-91 to 1999-2000	14.03	8.99	5.04	0.87	0.98
2000-01 to 2009-10	15.19	9.63	5.56	1.12	1.17
2010-11 to 2016-17	16.60	10.36	6.24	1.2	1.06
1970-71 to 2016-17	14.35	9.29	5.04	1.17	1.18

Source: *Handbook of Statistics on Indian Economy* & *State Finances: A Study of Budgets*, RBI, various issues.

2016-17 (Table 2.3). In other words, a higher growth rate of GDP had not translated into a larger revenue base. The buoyancy of own tax revenue at the all-States level has been higher than that of the Centre during this period, except during 2010-11 to 2016-17. The

Figure 2.1: Share of interest receipts in non-tax revenue–GDP ratio, 1970-71 to 2016-17

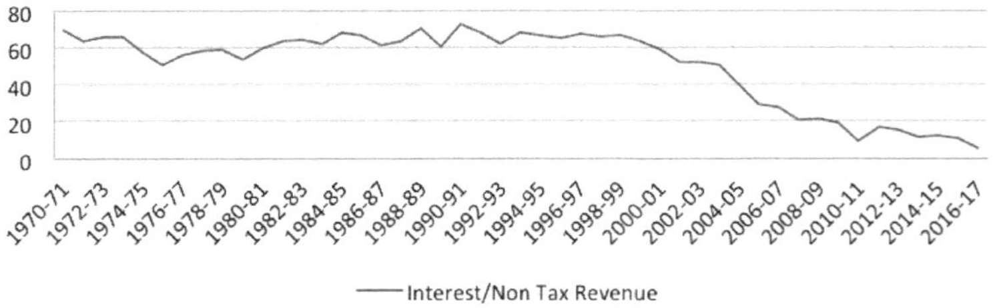

Source: *Handbook of Statistics on Indian Economy*, RBI, various issues.

post-2011 trend is due to a fall in buoyancy to less than unity for the States since 2013-14. The persistent low buoyancy is due to a general economic slowdown and to the shocks imparted by central policies like demonetization, which are beyond the control of the State governments. But overall, the performance of the States has been better than that of the Centre, though the former have taxes that are much less buoyant in their domain.

The average own tax revenue to GDP ratio of all States during 1970-71 to 2016-17 was 5.04 per cent while that for the gross tax revenue of Centre was 9.29 per cent (Table 2.3). While the Centre's tax to GDP ratio increased from 8.23 per cent of GDP to 10.36 per cent of GDP during this period, States' own tax to GDP ratio rose from 3.83 per cent to 6.24 per cent. In other words, States' own tax to GDP ratio had almost doubled during this period. The revenue expenditure to GDP ratio of all States also increased from 8.34 to 12.75 per cent (Table 2.1). Though the own tax revenue of the States rose, the revenue gap between the Centre and the States has widened over this period. But, the expenditure gap between these two tiers of government has not changed much, which points to the vertical fiscal imbalances between the Centre and the States (Table 2.2). This suggests that the States need a higher proportion of taxes to be devolved from the Centre so that the vertical fiscal imbalances are ameliorated.

Table 2.4: Non-tax revenue–GDP ratios of Centre and States, 1970-71 to 2016-17

Period	Average non-tax revenue-GDP ratio	Share of interest receipts in Centre's non-tax revenue	States' own non-tax revenue-GDP ratio
1970-71 to 1979-80	1.96	60.04	1.68
1980-81 to 1989-90	2.29	64.16	1.85
1990-91 to 1999-2000	2.39	66.92	1.68
2000-01 to 2009-10	2.31	36.96	1.4
2010–11 to 2016-17	1.85	12.31	1.15
1970-71 to 2016-17	2.18	50.21	1.58

Source: *Handbook of Statistics on Indian Economy*, RBI, various issues.

A. Non-Tax Revenues

The major component of non-tax revenue of the Centre has been interest receipts, but its share has been declining markedly. This is due to a fall in the central loans to the States after the discontinuation of the practice of on-lending to the States by the Centre, based on the recommendations of the 12th FC. The trends in non-tax revenues and interest receipts are depicted in Table 2.4 and Figure 2.1. In the case of the States, the own non-tax revenue to GDP ratio has been showing a decline since the 1990s. Since, most of the services in the State List are in social and economic sectors that are availed of by the poor and lower-income groups, raising non-tax revenues through enhanced user charges on those services would be politically infeasible as well as economically unviable. As a share of total revenue receipts of the States, non-tax revenues amount to less than 10 per cent and cannot be a very buoyant source of receipts like tax revenue.

B. Resources Transfer from the Centre

The ratio of central taxes transferred to and grants made to the States to GDP declined during the 1990s and recorded a marginal increase during the first decade of this century. During the second decade of 2010-11 to 2016-17, the share of central taxes devolved

Table 2.5: Average central transfers–GDP

Period	Central tax share–GDP ratio	Central grant share–GDP ratio
1970-71 to 1979-80	1.83	1.57
1980-81 to 1989-90	2.46	1.92
1990-95 to 1999-2000	2.43	1.86
2000-01 to 2009-10	2.54	1.99
2010-11 to 2014-15	2.84	2.12
2015-16to 2016-17	3.13	2.36
1970-71 to 2016-17	2.43	1.91

Source: *Handbook of Statistics on Indian Economy*, RBI, various issues.

to the states (relative to GDP) went up (Table 2.5). This is mainly due to enhanced tax devolution in the initial two years (2015-16 and 2016-17) of the 14th FC award. If we compare the period 2010-11 to 2014-15, with that of the previous five yearly period, 2005-06 to 2009-10, the increase in tax devolution to States is marginal from 2.76 to 2.84 per cent of GDP. During 2015-16 and 2016-17, central tax share to GDP ratio went up to 3.70 and 3.85 per cent respectively. There has also been a rise in the central grants to GDP ratio over 2010-11 to 2016-17. But the point to be noted here is that, in 2014-15, there was a change in the method of grants transfer to the States. The entire central share in CSS was routed through the State budgets instead of being given directly to the implementation agencies as was done till then. This explains the rise in the share of grants relative to GDP during 2014-15 to 2.66 per cent as against 1.83 and 1.90 per cent during 2012-13 and 2013-14 respectively. In fact, figures prior to and in 2014-15 are not strictly comparable. There is a decline in the grant–GDP ratio during 2015-16 and 2016-17 to 2.38 and 2.35 per cent respectively due to a fall in the central share in many of the CSS.

TRENDS IN REVENUE EXPENDITURE: 1970-71 TO 2016-17

There has been an increase in the revenue expenditure to GDP ratio of the Centre from 8.06 per cent during the 1970s to 12.24 per

Table 2.6: Ratio of major central revenue expenditure to GDP (%)

Period	Defence	Interest	Subsidies
1970-71 to 1979-80	2.41	1.46	0.73
1980-81 to 1989-90	2.33	2.53	1.53
1990-91 to 1999-2000	1.64	4.12	1.35
2000-01 to 2009-10	1.41	3.94	1.57
2010-11 to 2016-17	1.12	3.18	2.19

Source: *Handbook of Statistics on Indian Economy*, RBI, various issues.

Figure 2.2: Defence, interest and subsidies as ratio to GDP (Centre), 1970-71 to 2016-17

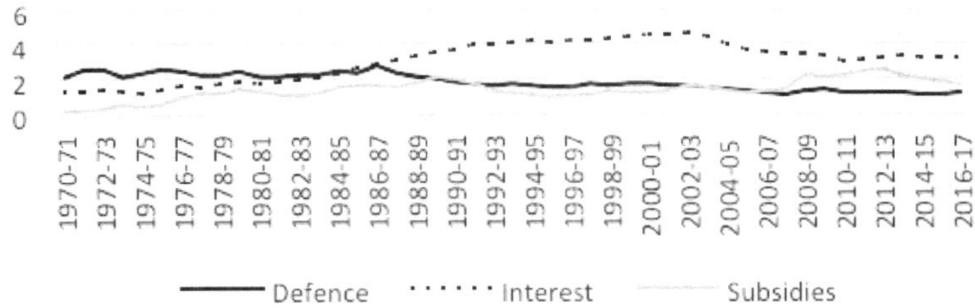

Source: *Handbook of Statistics on Indian Economy*, RBI, various issues.

cent during 2010-11 to 2016-17. As regards the States, the ratio has risen from 8.34 per cent to 12.75 per cent during the same period (Table 2.2). Among the components of revenue expenditure of the Centre, defence has shown a declining trend, whereas interest and subsidies have shown a rising trend (Table 2.6). The interest expenditure of the Centre has risen through the decades due to an increase in the volume of borrowings and resorting to (higher interest) market borrowing since 1994 by converting the existing 91-day treasury bills into dated Government securities. After the 1990s, there has been moderation in the interest expenditure to GDP ratio due to the lower interest rate regime. The ratio of defence expenditure to GDP has declined while that of subsidies has shown an increase. The revenue expenditure to GDP ratio rose during the 1980s (Table 2.2), when government spending increased and revenue deficits became endemic in central finance. The second spurt in revenue expenditure was over 2000-01 to 2009-

Table 2.7: Central and States' share in development expenditure, 1990-91 to 2016-17 (%)

Year	Central share in combined development expenditure	States' share in combined development expenditure
1990-91	39.67	60.33
1995-96	35.81	64.19
1996-97	34.55	64.45
1997-98	36.01	63.99
1998-99	35.42	64.58
1999-2000	35.47	64.53
2000-01	36.84	63.16
2001-02	37.46	62.54
2002-03	41.06	58.94
20003-04	40.02	59.98
2004-05	40.10	59.10
2005-06	42.57	57.43
2006-07	43.36	56.64
2007-08	46.29	53.71
2008-09	50.85	49.15
2009-10	57.31	52.29
2010-11	48.46	52.54
2011-12	47.43	52.57
2012-13	43.13	56.87
2013-14	39.78	60.22
2014-15	36.74	63.26
2015-16	35.78	64.22
2016-17	34.81	65.19

Source: *Indian Public Finance Statistics*, *Finance Accounts of the Union*, various issues.

10, because a fiscal stimulus was provided to counter the crisis-induced economic slowdown since 2007-08. However, due to the constraints imposed by FRBM Acts, States have not undertaken counter-cyclical spending even during this slowdown phase of the economy.

At the State level, development expenditure, which includes social sector spending on education and health, is dominant. Within the development expenditure of the States, social sector spending constitutes 63.77 per cent of the total as against 36.23 per cent for economic services during 1990-91 to 2016-17.

Figure 2.3: Development revenue expenditure components of Centre and States

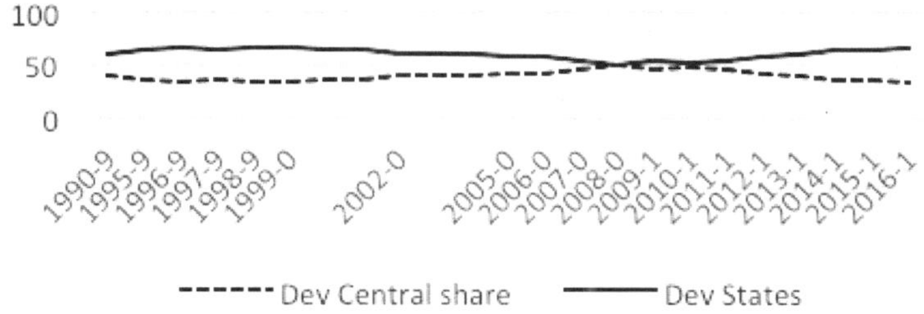

Source: *Indian Public Finance Statistics* and *State Finances: A Study of Budgets*, various issues.

As a proportion of combined revenue expenditure, development expenditure of all States amounted to 59.66 per cent during the period 1990-91 to 2016-17, as compared with a lower 40.34 per cent for the Centre. The central share of development expenditure rose to marginally exceed that of the States in 2008-09 (50.85 and 49.15 per cent respectively), but later fell to 34.81 per cent as against 65.19 per cent for all States during 2016-17 (Table 2.7 and Figure 2.3). The share of development expenditure of the Centre in the combined development expenditure of the Centre and the States was on an average 36.15 per cent during the 1990s. This rose steadily after 2005-06 from 42.57 per cent to 50.85 per cent during 2008-09. This rise was due to the launch of the national flagship employment programme (following the passing of the Mahatma Gandhi National Rural Employment Guarantee Act – MGNREGA[3]) and other social sector schemes. However, the central share fell consistently after that and has been around 35 per cent since 2014-15 due to small incremental allocations as well as a fall in the central share in the CSS.

TRENDS IN CAPITAL EXPENDITURE: 1970-71 TO 2016-17

Capital expenditure as a proportion of GDP showed a declining

[3] The initial name was National Rural Employment Guarantee Act (NREGA), which was later renamed MGNREGA.

Table 2.8: Trends in capital expenditure, 1970-71 to 2016-17

Period	Capital expenditure –GDP ratio of Centre and States	Capital expenditure –GDP ratio of Centre	Capital expenditure –GDP ratio of all States
1970-71 to 1979-80	7.39	5.8	1.59
1980-81 to 1989-90	7.88	6.01	1.87
1990-91 to 1999-2000	5.05	3.64	1.41
2000-01 to 2009-10	4.3	2.36	1.94
2010–11 to 2016-17	4.03	1.78	2.25
1970-71 to 2016-17	5.83	4.05	1.78

Source: *Handbook of Statistics on Indian Economy*, RBI, various issues.

trend since the 1990s at the central level (Table 2.8). It has declined from 5.80 per cent during the 1970s to 1.78 per cent during 2010-11 to 2016-17. The recent decline in capital spending at the central level can be attributed to the discontinuation of on-lending to States. Also, a large part of capital spending is done through various off-budget borrowings. In the case of States, the capital expenditure to GDP ratio went up starting in the 2000s. This is the consequence of the decline in the revenue deficit of the States, which helped the them to spend the borrowed money for capital spending.

TRENDS IN FISCAL AND REVENUE DEFICITS: 1970-71 TO 2016-17

It can be seen from Table 2.9 that improvement in two major deficit indicators, fiscal and revenue deficit to GDP ratio has been better at the all-States level when compared to that of the Centre. The States had almost achieved balance in their revenue account during the period 2010-11 to 2016-17, which enabled them to earmark nearly the entire borrowings for capital expenditure, while the Centre had spent 69.05 per cent of its borrowings on revenue expenditure. States had brought down their fiscal deficit to GDP ratio to below 3 per cent, whereas that deficit has remained consistently above 3 per cent for the Centre. In the case of the

Table 2.9: FD, RD and RD/FD of Centre and States, 1970-71 to 2016-17

Period	Centre + States FD/GDP	Centre + States RD/GDP	Centre + States RD/FD	Centre FD/GDP	Centre RD/GDP	Centre RD/FD	States FD/GDP	States RD/GDP	States RD/FD
1970-71 to 1979-80	5.61	-0.85	-41.95	3.67	-0.29	-9.5	1.94	-0.56	-32.45
1980-81 to 1989-90	9.32	1.59	19.75	6.56	1.67	24.28	2.76	-0.08	-4.53
1990-91 to 1999-2000	8.72	4.09	87.65	5.72	2.93	51.48	3	1.16	36.17
2000-01 to 2009-10	7.83	4.33	87.51	4.77	3.35	67.61	3.06	0.98	19.9
2010–11 to 2016-17	7	3.165	68.1	4.52	3.16	69.05	2.48	0.005	-0.95
1970-71 to 2016-17	7.74	2.42	42.69	5.08	2.1	38.77	2.66	0.32	3.92

Source: *Handbook of Statistics on Indian Economy*, RBI, various issues.

Figure 2.4: Central and all States fiscal deficit–GDP Ratio, 1970-71 to 2016-17

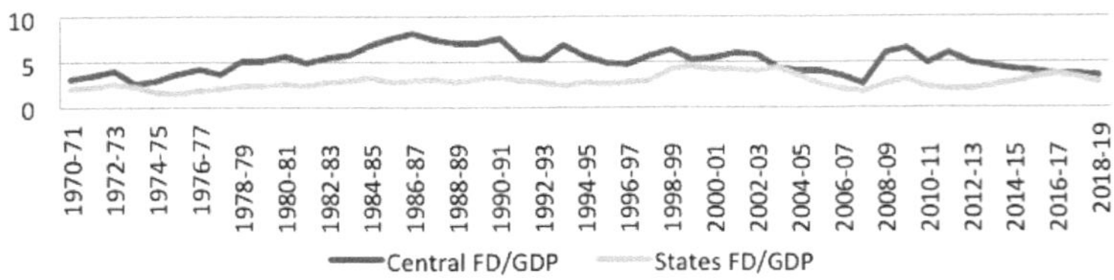

Source: *Handbook of Statistics on Indian Economy*, RBI, various issues.

Figure 2.5: Central and all States revenue deficit–GDP ratio, 1970-71 to 2016-17

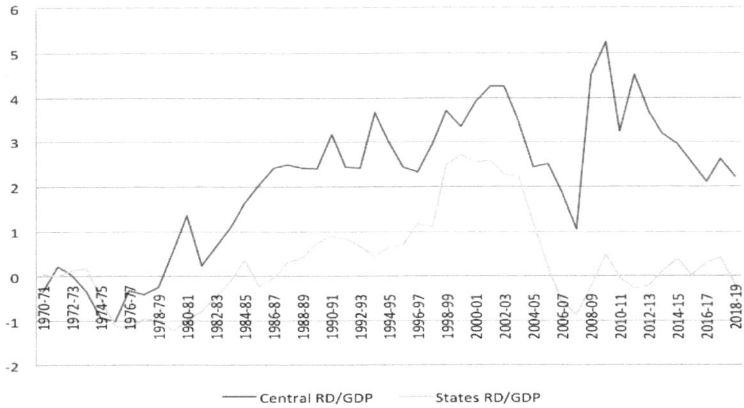

Source: *Handbook of Statistics on Indian Economy*, RBI, various issues.

primary deficit (fiscal deficit net of interest payments) to GDP ratio also, the States showed better performance, except in two recent years, when their capital spending and borrowing under the Ujwal DISCOM Assurance Yojana (UDAY) to take over losses of power transmission companies resulted in an increase of the primary deficit. Overall, the deficit indicators have shown much better improvement at the all-States level when compared to that of the Centre (Table 2.9, Figures 2.4, 2.5, 2.6 and 2.7). This is mainly due to the fact that the States have been compelled to adhere to FRBM targets by successive FCs since the 11th by linking central grants and

Figure 2.6: Central and all States primary deficit–GDP ratio, 1970-71 to 2016-17

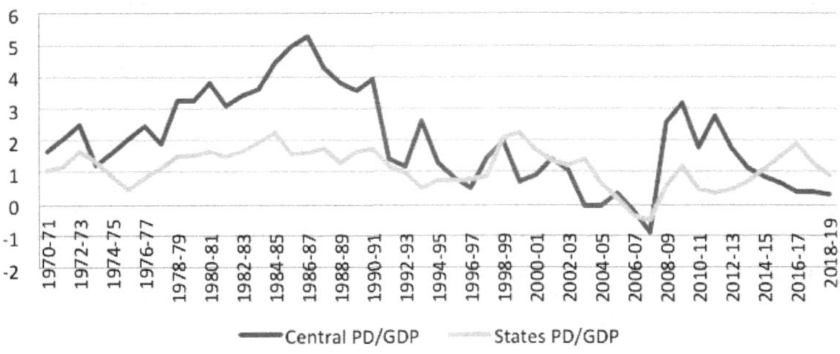

Source: *Handbook of Statistics on Indian Economy*, RBI, various issues.

Figure 2.7: Central and all States capital expenditure–GDP ratio, 1970-71 to 2016-17

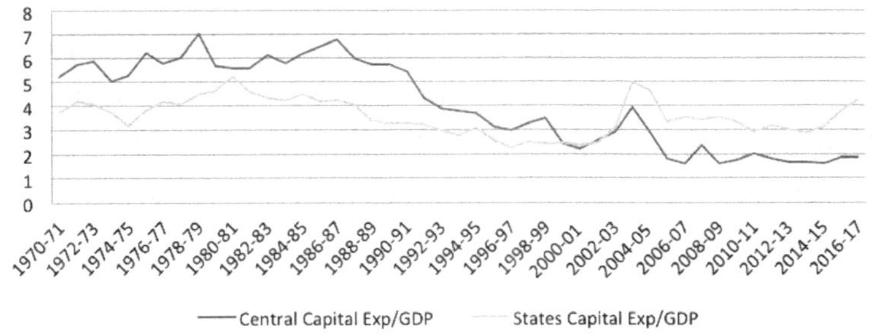

Source: *Handbook of Statistics on Indian Economy*, RBI, various issues.

debt relief to achieving these targets. This has, however, resulted in perverse incentives like inefficient use of borrowed funds by the States which we discuss later in this chapter.

TRENDS IN BORROWINGS AND LIABILITIES: 1980-81 TO 2016-17

At the central level, under the heads of borrowings and liabilities, the major component is internal debt followed by small savings and others and external liabilities. The share of internal

Table 2.8: Trends in capital expenditure, 1970-71 to 2016-17

Period	Capital expenditure –GDP ratio of Centre and States	Capital expenditure –GDP ratio of Centre	Capital expenditure –GDP ratio of all States
1970-71 to 1979-80	7.39	5.8	1.59
1980-81 to 1989-90	7.88	6.01	1.87
1990-91 to 1999-2000	5.05	3.64	1.41
2000-01 to 2009-10	4.3	2.36	1.94
2010–11 to 2016-17	4.03	1.78	2.25
1970-71 to 2016-17	5.83	4.05	1.78

Source: *Handbook of Statistics on Indian Economy*, RBI, various issues.

debt, which comprises market borrowings, 91-day, 182-day and 364-day treasury bills, has gone up with a corresponding decline in small savings and external liabilities (Table 2.10). The borrowings and liabilities of the Centre as a ratio of GDP rose during the 1990s and the first decade of the 2000s and came down during the period 2010-11 to 2016-17. For the financial year 2016-17, the latest year for which budget actuals are available, the ratio is at 50.30 per cent. As regards composition, the share of external liabilities has been coming down.

At the State level too, the components of borrowings and liabilities have undergone a change. States are now depending more on market borrowing. The share of internal debt, out of which market borrowing is a major component has been rising from 15.11 per cent of the total liabilities during the 1980s to 68.75 per cent during 2010-11 to 2016-17. The share of loans from the Centre has come down from 61.52 per cent during 1980s to 6.13 per cent during 2010-11 to 2016-17 (Table 2.11). This is due to the implementation of the recommendations of the 12th FC to transfer external loans on the same conditions to the States. The share of provident funds and other accounts, which are in the Public Account has increased from 23.37 per cent during the 1980s to 26.19 per cent during 2010-11 to 2016-17. At the all-States level, the ratio of borrowings and liabilities to GDP has come down during

Table 2.9 FD, RD and RD/FD of Centre and States, 1970-71 to 2016-17

Period	Centre + States FD/GDP	Centre + States RD/GDP	Centre + States RD/FD	Centre FD/GDP	Centre RD/GDP	Centre RD/FD	States FD/GDP	States RD/GDP	States RD/FD
1970-71 to 1979-80	5.61	-0.85	-41.95	3.67	-0.29	-9.5	1.94	-0.56	-32.45
1980-81 to 1989-90	9.32	1.59	19.75	6.56	1.67	24.28	2.76	-0.08	-4.53
1990-91 to 1999-2000	8.72	4.09	87.65	5.72	2.93	51.48	3	1.16	36.17
2000-01 to 2009-10	7.83	4.33	87.51	4.77	3.35	67.61	3.06	0.98	19.9
2010–11 to 2016-17	7	3.165	68.1	4.52	3.16	69.05	2.48	0.005	-0.95
1970-71 to 2016-17	7.74	2.42	42.69	5.08	2.1	38.77	2.66	0.32	3.92

Source: *Handbook of Statistics on Indian Economy*, RBI, various issues.

Table 2.10: Borrowings and liabilities of Centre and States, 1970-71 to 2016-17

Period	Borrowings & liabilities–GDP ratio, Centre	External liabilities–total liabilities, Centre	Borrowings & liabilities–GDP ratio, all States
1980-81 to 1989-90	47.97	16.35	20.15
1990-91 to 1999-2000	58.89	20.79	21.71
2000-01 to 2009-10	62.02	9.63	29.22
2010–11 to 2016-17	52	6.21	22.74
1980-81 to 2016-17	55.48	13.81	23.51

Source: *Handbook of Statistics on Indian Economy*, RBI, various issues.

Table 2.11: Components of borrowings and liabilities of all States, 1980-81 to 2016-17

Period	Internal debt	Loans from Centre	Provident funds and other deposits	Market borrowings	Ways & means advance (WMA) from RBI
1980-81 to 1989-90	15.11	61.52	23.37	10.64	0.09
1990-91 to 1999-2000	17.65	52.64	29.71	14.18	0.03
2000-01 to 2009-10	51.15	22.59	26.25	21.26	0.63
2010–11 to 2016-17	68.75	6.13	25.12	42.95	1.01*
1980-81 to 2016-17	35.69	38.12	26.19	20.58	0.39

Source: *Handbook of Statistics on Indian Economy*, RBI, various issues.

Note: Market borrowings and WMA from RBI are components of Internal Debt along with Special Securities issued to NSSF and Compensation Bonds. The increase is due to revised and budget estimates for 2015-16 and 2016-17 in which WMA from RBI is estimated at 3.75 and 3.30 per cent of Total Liabilities. During 2010-11 to 2014-15, it is zero.

Figure 2.8: Components of Central borrowings and liabilities, 1980-81 to 2016-17

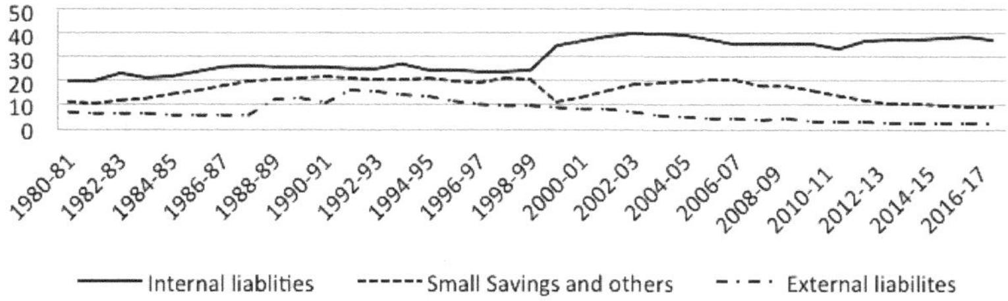

Source: *Handbook of Statistics on Indian Economy*, RBI, various issues.

Figure 2.9: Borrowings and liabilities of Centre as a ratio of GDP, 1980-81 to 2016-17

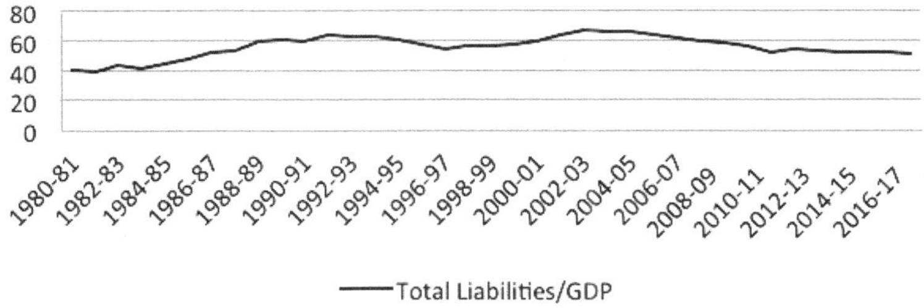

Source: *Handbook of Statistics on Indian Economy*, RBI, various issues.

Figure 2.10: Borrowings and liabilities of all States as a ratio of GDP, 1980-81 to 2016-17

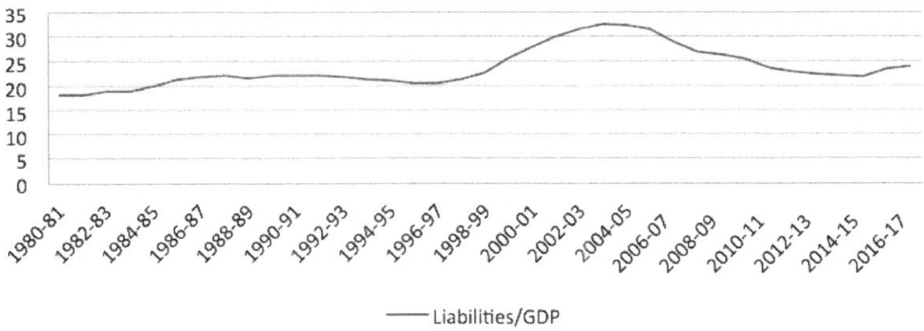

Source: *Handbook of Statistics on Indian Economy*, RBI, various issues.

2010-11 to 2016-17 to 22.74 per cent from 29.22 per cent during 2000-01 to 2009-10 (Table 2.10).

Thus, if we take a holistic view of fiscal consolidation, the performance of the States has been better than that of the Centre. The quality of the deficit, proxied by the ratio of the revenue to the fiscal deficit has been far less for the States. The States have almost balanced their revenue accounts unlike the Centre. The primary deficit to GDP ratio of all States has been higher than that of the Centre only during the last two financial years due to the higher capital expenditure–GDP ratio for all States together. Keeping this in mind, any future fiscal consolidation framework should provide sufficient fiscal space for capital expenditure at the State level. It would be in the fairness of things, that given the ceilings in the FRBM framework, unless the Centre adheres to its targets, States would be forced to bear a disproportionate burden of fiscal targeting, which would lead to a reduction in their fiscal space for development spending. It is in this background that we examine the trends in vertical fiscal imbalances between the Centre and the States in Chapter 3.

CHAPTER 3

WORSENING VERTICAL FISCAL IMBALANCE

As we have underlined in our discussions earlier, the basic issue in Centre–State relations relates to the vertical fiscal imbalance between resource endowments and expenditure obligations of the Centre and States. The own resources available to the State governments is inadequate to meet their expenditure requirements. In order to mitigate this imbalance, in every federation there exists some system of resource transfer to the regional governments. In the present chapter, we discuss issues that are important to the system of tax devolution and grant disbursement in India.

What has been the trend in the vertical imbalance before tax devolution? Has the tax devolution been adequate to mitigate these imbalances or what has been the trend in the vertical imbalance after tax devolution? And how has the tax devolution awarded by the FCs been eroded by the manipulation of the size of the divisible pool?

The sharp increase in vertical imbalances is reflected in the rising pre-devolution resource gap of the State governments (Table 3.1). The gap is defined as the difference between States' own tax resources and State government expenditure. The pre-devolution gap which was 2.41 per cent of GDP in 1950-51 widened steadily to peak at 9.19 per cent in 1987-88. Since then it has declined and remained relatively stable at around 8 per cent. In 2014-15 and 2015-16, it exceeded 10 per cent.

Table 3.1: Central transfers and pre- and post-devolution resource gap of states (% of GDP)

Year	States' own tax revenues	Central transfers tax devolution	Total State tax revenues	State expenditure	Pre-devolution gap	Post-devolution gap
1950-51	2.13	0.46	2.60	4.55	2.41	1.95
1960-61	2.54	0.92	3.46	8.18	5.65	4.73
1970-71	3.25	1.58	4.83	9.12	5.88	4.29
1980-81	4.45	2.53	6.99	12.96	8.50	5.97
1981-82	4.72	2.43	7.15	12.40	7.68	5.25
1982-83	4.85	2.36	7.21	12.89	8.03	5.67
1983-84	4.72	2.29	7.01	12.83	8.12	5.83
1984-85	4.81	2.25	7.06	13.46	8.65	6.39
1985-86	5.04	2.59	7.63	13.72	8.67	6.09
1986-87	5.16	2.62	7.77	14.00	8.84	6.23
1987-88	5.24	2.61	7.85	14.44	9.19	6.59
1988-89	5.14	2.44	7.58	13.62	8.48	6.04
1989-90	5.19	2.64	7.83	13.68	8.49	5.85
1990-91	5.14	2.48	7.62	13.87	8.73	6.25
1991-92	5.32	2.55	7.87	14.38	9.06	6.51
1992-93	5.10	2.65	7.75	13.94	8.84	6.19
1993-94	5.19	2.50	7.68	13.70	8.51	6.02
1994-95	5.31	2.38	7.69	13.92	8.60	6.23
1995-96	5.22	2.39	7.61	13.35	8.13	5.74
1996-97	5.02	2.47	7.49	12.97	7.95	5.48
1997-98	5.18	2.77	7.95	13.32	8.14	5.37
1998-99	4.95	2.17	7.12	13.71	8.76	6.59
1999-00	5.08	2.15	7.23	14.47	9.38	7.23
2000-01	5.36	2.39	7.75	14.09	8.72	6.34
2001-02	5.41	2.27	7.68	14.48	9.07	6.81
2002-03	5.53	2.21	7.75	14.27	8.74	6.52
2003.04	5.62	2.37	7.99	15.13	9.51	7.14
2004-05	5.84	2.47	8.31	14.34	8.50	6.03
2005-06	6.00	2.60	8.59	14.14	8.15	5.55
2006-07	6.13	2.85	8.98	14.42	8.29	5.44
2007-08	5.56	3.08	8.64	13.34	7.78	4.70
2008-09	5.51	2.88	8.39	13.84	8.33	5.45
2009-10	5.81	2.59	8.40	14.76	8.95	6.36
2010-11	6.15	2.87	9.02	14.01	7.86	5.00
2011-12	6.43	2.88	9.31	13.98	7.55	4.67
2012-13	6.72	2.91	9.63	14.29	7.57	4.65
2013-14 (PE)	6.52	2.84	9.36	14.23	7.71	4.87
2014-15	6.79	2.75	9.54	17.39	10.60	7.85
2015-16 2nd RE	7.04	3.85	10.89	17.05	10.01	6.16

Source: *Indian Public Finance Statistics.*

Note: GDP is at current market price from 2004-05 and 2011-12 series.

Table 3.1(a): Decadal average of pre- and post-devolution resource gap (% to GDP)

1980-81 to 1989-90	8.47	5.99
1990-91 to 1999-2000	8.61	6.16
2000-01 to 2009-10	8.60	6.03
2010-11 to 2016-17	8.80	5.67

Source: Table 3.1.

Figure 3.1: Central transfers, pre- and post-tax devolution gaps, 1950-51 to 2016-17 (% of GDP)

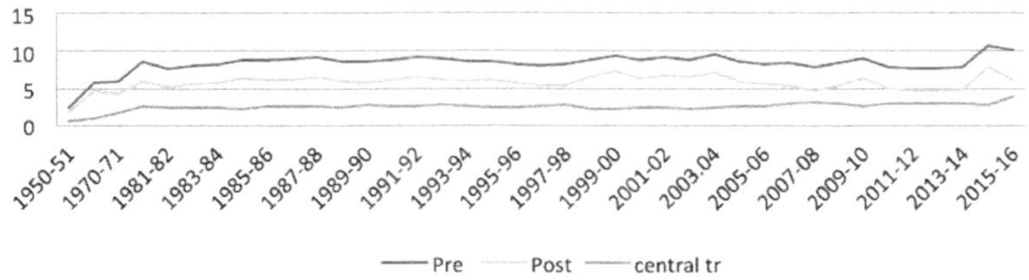

Source: Table 3.1.

As is discernible from Table 3.1(a), the pre-devolution gap has not declined since the 1980s. During the last period, (2010-11 to 2016-17), it rose by 0.20 per cent. As regards post-devolution gap, it has arisen during the 1990s and had a marginal decline during the first decade of 2000s, but was still higher than that during the 1980s. The decline in post-devolution gap during the period 2010-11 to 2016-17 to 5.67 per cent is due to the higher tax devolution by the 14th FC. But it needs to be mentioned that pre and post devolution gaps went up during 2015-16 and 2016-17 to 10.2 and 11 per cent and 6.5 and 7 per cent respectively as against 8.08 and 5.24 respectively for pre and post devolution gaps during 2010-11 to 2014-15. This is a clear indication of worsening of vertical fiscal imbalances despite higher tax devolution by the 14th FC.

CSS AND VERTICAL FISCAL IMBALANCES: AN OVERVIEW

The above discussion on the vertical fiscal imbalance tends to understate the gravity of the problem because the ex-post figure of

Figure 3.1: Central transfers, pre- and post-tax devolution gaps, 1950-51 to 2016-17 (% of GDP)

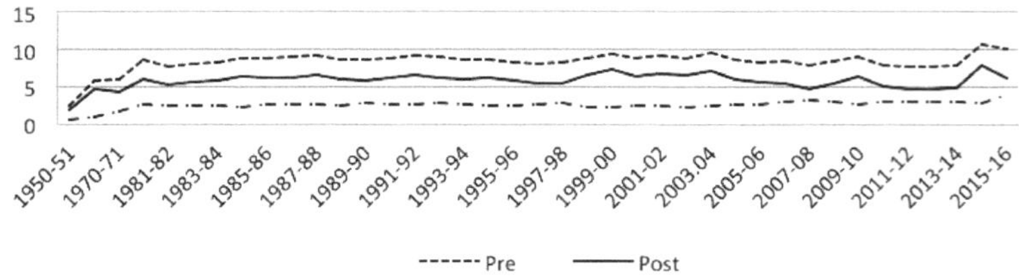

Source: Table 3.1

state expenditures does not fully reflect the functional responsibility of the States, given the fiscal constraint imposed by inadequate revenues and the functions taken over by the Centre through CSS. A rough indicator of this may be gleaned from the quantum of resources devolved through CSS in areas which are by and large within the functional domain of the State governments. The 14th FC has observed that 'between 2002-05 and 2005-11, revenue expenditure by the Union Government on State List subjects increased from an average of 14 per cent to 20 per cent and on Concurrent List subjects from an average of 13 per cent to 17 per cent. This implies a reduction in expenditure in percentage terms on Union List subjects. Expenditure functions under the Union List fall predominantly under General and Economic Services. The share of expenditure on these has progressively declined from 66.3 per cent in 2001-02 to 53.2 per cent in 2014-15 (BE)' (14th FC Report, para 6.17). This implies that the Union government is encroaching into the functional domain of the States and competing with the latter in an overlapping functional space.

Two issues that are relevant here are the impact of various central level legislations on State finances and the implications of counterpart funding through various CSS, especially various flagship schemes. There are several flagship programmes where large sums of resources are allocated by the central government. During the 12th Five-Year Plan period, 1,016 central sector schemes and 147 CSS (of which 16 are flagship schemes) were under operation. The expenditure on flagship schemes as a percentage of GDP increased from 2.93 per cent to 3.43 per cent between 2007-08 and 2011-12. States' expenditure on CSS/flagship schemes as matching contributions has also sharply increased as a result. This led to a shrinkage in the fiscal space in which the States determine their expenditure based on their own priorities.

The B.K. Chaturvedi Committee (2011) on restructuring of CSS highlighted the fact that Normal Central Assistance (NCA) to States, which is formula-based, as a percentage of Gross Budgetary Support (GBS) was only 6.74 per cent during the 11th Plan period. This implied that the share of untied grants for financing of State plans was meagre. The committee recommended weeding out and restructuring schemes into flagship schemes, major sub-sectoral schemes and umbrella schemes and operational flexibility based on the development gaps within a specific area. Later, the report of a sub-group of chief ministers (GoI 2015a) also made suggestions for restructuring of CSS. Since then, there has been restructuring of CSS into 'core of core', 'core' and 'optional' schemes, but States' share in most of the schemes, i.e. in the 'core' category, has gone up from 25 to 40 per cent and the much talked about operational flexibility is still a mirage.

Though there have been attempts to reform the CSS, it appears from the ToR of the 15th FC that the central government is keen on bringing back conditional grants as a major component in the scheme of central transfers to the States. It would be relevant to quote here an observation made in an editorial in the *Economic and Political Weekly* titled 'Uncooperative Federalism' (Volume 53, No. 15, April 14, 2018):

> The 14th FC was the first to take an aggregate view of resources and expenditures, and recommend 42% tax devolution to cover both

Table 3.2: Proportion of surcharges and cesses to gross tax revenue (%)

Year (1)	Gross tax revenue (GTR) (2) (Rs crore)	Surcharges and cesses (3) (Rs crore)	(3) as a % of (2)
2011-12	8,89,176	57,498	6.47
2012-13	10,26,234	59,569	5.80
2013-14	11,38,733	66,411	5.83
2014-15	12,44,884	74,399	5.98
2015-16	14,55,648	82,510	5.67
2016-17	17,15,822	1,10,710	6.45
2017-18 RE	19,46,119	1,39,261	7.16
2018-19 BE	22,71,242	2,78,028	12.24

Source: Budget Documents of the Union Government.
Note: Surcharges and cesses exclude the GST cess.

Table 3.3: Shared taxes in divisible pool, 2000-01 to 2016-17

Finance Commission (1)	Period (2)	Central transfers as % of gross revenue receipts (3)	Share of net proceeds recommended and accepted (%) (4)	Gap (3) – (4) (%)
Eleventh	2000-01 to 2004-05	26.97	29.5	2.53
Twelfth	2005-06 to 2009-10	26.32	30.5	4.18
Thirteenth	1995-00	28.24	32	3.76
Fourteenth (till 2016-17)	2000-05	34.13	42	7.87

Source: Budget Documents of the Union and Reports of the Finance Commissions.

non-plan and plan revenue expenditures of states. At the same time, the 14th FC's assessment of Union finances from 2015-16 to 2019-20 provided sufficient fiscal resources for the Union to perform functions listed in the Union list and on national development priorities reflected through CSS. However, in an unprecedented mandate, the 15th FC has been asked to review the impact of enhanced tax devolution recommended by the 14th FC on the fiscal situation of the Union government along with the continuing imperative of the national development programme, including New India-2022. . . . This New India initiative may also proliferate CSS in social and economic sectors. Further, in a federal system, where State governments are responsible for spending around 58% of the combined expenditure of the Union and States, can any national development agenda be set by cutting the flow of resources to States? The implication of the ToR is loud and clear. The Union government is keen to reverse the process of greater fiscal autonomy and have greater control over state resources and functions.

INCREASING VERTICAL IMBALANCE AND RISING NON-DIVISIBLE POOL OF CENTRAL REVENUES

In this section, we highlight how the central government is using various taxation instruments in a way that goes against the spirit of the Constitution to deny the States their rightful share of national taxes. As per the constitutional provision of Article 271, surcharges and cesses imposed by the Union government are not shareable with the States. In recent years, continuous increase in cess and surcharges is reducing the share of divisible pool of revenues and increasing the non-divisible part that is retained by the central government. The surcharges and cesses are increasing as a proportion of gross tax revenue of the Centre from 6.47 per cent in 2011-12 to 12.24 per cent in 2018-19 budget estimates (Table 3.2).

As evident from Table 3.3, the difference between the share of taxes recommended by the FC as a percentage of net proceeds [gross tax revenue – ((surcharges and cesses) + cost of collection)] and share of taxes devolved as a percentage of gross tax revenue of the Centre is increasing sharply in recent years. The gap between the two is highest during the award period of the 14th FC, during which it was claimed the devolution had been enhanced substantially. It may not be wrong to conclude that a substantial part of the enhanced devolution by the 14th FC was offset by measures like those noted above and by the restructuring of central grants to States.

Various FCs have suggested that surcharges and cesses are to be levied for specific purposes for a limited period. There is a need

Table 3.4: Loss to States from levy of surcharges and cesses (in Rs crore)

Year	GTR	Cost of collection	Net proceeds without surcharges	Divisible Pool at 42 per cent of (4)	Actual Divisible Pool	Loss due to surcharges and cesses
2015-16	14,55,648	9,260	14,46,388	6,07,483	5,06,192	1,01,291
2016-17	17,15,822	11,472	17,04,350	7,15,827	6,08,000	1,07,827
2017-18 RE	19,46,119	14,350	19,31,769	8,11,343	6,73,005	1,38,338
2018-19 BE	22,71,242	14,805	22,56,437	9,47,704	7,68,412	1,79,292
						5,26,747

Source: Budget Documents of the Union.

to merge surcharges and cesses which continue for a long time, say more than two years, with the basic taxes and made shareable with the States.

In the last two Union budgets, surcharges and cesses are being used as mechanisms to shrink the divisible pool of taxes and compensate the Centre for the perceived loss of revenue due to enhanced devolution. In the 2017-18 budget, the rate of income tax upto Rs 5 lakh was reduced from 10 per cent to 5 per cent and the revenue loss was sought to be compensated by levering a surcharge on taxes on incomes above Rs 50 lakh. Had this been done by raising the slab rates, the divisible pool would not have become smaller. In the 2018-19 budget, the excise duty on petroleum products was reduced by Rs 9 per litre but road cess, which is not shareable with the States, was increased by an equivalent amount. These attempts to truncate the divisible pool of taxes, shareable with the States defeats the constitutional scheme to ameliorate vertical imbalances. Table 3.4 clearly shows that as the share of taxes to the States recommended by the FCs went up, the gap between the gross tax revenues and net proceeds increased.

This points to a conscious effort to retain and exacerbate the vertical imbalances by indirectly defeating the spirit of FC recommendations on sharing of taxes. The financial loss to the

States is also not negligible. During the period 2015-16 to 2018-19 BE, the divisible pool shrank by Rs 5,26,747 crore (Table 3.4), which is an average of about 3 per cent of the Gross Domestic Product at current prices.

In this context, the observations of the Justice M.M. Punchhi Commission on Centre–State Relations (2010, Volume III, pp. 55-56) is pertinent. The relevant portion of the report is extracted below:

> 6.3.01 The 80th Amendment of the Constitution provided for the sharing of all Union taxes between the Centre and the States except the proceeds of taxes referred to in Articles 268 and 269 and the cesses and surcharges levied on Union taxes. This has met the long standing demand of the States for the enlargement of the divisible pool of central taxes. But the extension of the scope of cesses and surcharges imposed on central taxes has greatly reduced the divisible pool over the years. [. . .]
>
> 6.3.02 The introduction of new cesses and surcharges has neutralized the higher tax devolution recommended by the successive Finance Commissions. FC-XI and FC-XII recommended States' shares in net central taxes at 29.5 and 30.5 per cent, respectively. But because of large scale resort to the levy of cesses and surcharges, actual tax devolution to States were lower at 25.95 per cent of gross tax revenue in the award period of FC-XII as compared with tax devolution amounting to 26.57 per cent in the award period of FC-XI. Thus, the increase of States' share in central taxes by one percentage point by FC-XII was more than neutralized. The Finance Commissions' recommendations are based on the assessment of the resource position of the Centre and the States and their needs. Extension of cesses and surcharges amounts to dilution of the recommendations of the Finance Commissions and deprives the States of their due share in central tax revenue.

Table 3.5: Shortfall in net proceeds and taxes shareable with States (Rs crore)

Year	Gross tax revenues	Surcharges + cesses	Cost of collection	Net proceeds	States' share as per FC	Net proceeds as 100% of tax devolved	Discrepancy
2011-12	8,89,176	57,500	6,661	8,25,015	2,53,022	7,90,694	34,321
2012-13	10,26,234	59,572	7,303	9,59,359	2,91,546	9,11,081	48,278
2013-14	11,38,733	70,518	8,122	10,60,093	3,18,229	9,94,466	65,627
2014-15	12,44,884	74,401	8,796	11,61,687	3,37,808	10,55,650	1,06,037
2015-16	14,55,648	78,509	9,260	13,67,879	5,06,192	12,05,219	1,62,660
2016-17	17,15,822	1,23,318	11,472	15,81,032	6,08,000	14,47,619	1,33,413
2017-18 RE	19,46,119	1,37,510	14,350	17,94,259	6,73,005	16,02,393	1,91,866
2018-19 BE	22,71,242	2,85,917	14,805	19,70,520	7,68,412	18,29,552	1,40,968

Source: Budget Documents of the Union and Reports of the Finance Commissions.

It is necessary in the interests of reducing vertical imbalances that surcharges and cesses which are continuing for more than two financial years should be made part of the divisible pool and shared with the States and a Constitution amendment for this needs to be considered.

NON-TRANSPARENCY IN COMPUTATION OF NET PROCEEDS

Net proceeds are defined under Article 279 (1) of the Constitution as under:

> In the foregoing provisions of this Chapter, 'net proceeds' means in relation to any tax or duty the proceeds thereof reduced by the cost of collection, and for the purposes of those provisions the net proceeds of any tax or duty, or of any part of any tax or duty, in or attributable to any area shall be ascertained and certified by the Comptroller and Auditor-General of India, whose certificate shall be final.

As mentioned earlier, in short, net proceeds are gross tax revenue less the cost of collection and surcharges and cesses. But when computed from the budget documents of the Union, it can be seen that net proceeds are less than what they ought to have been. The computation is made as explained in this example. If Rs 100 is the share of States' taxes and 42 per cent of the net proceeds is prescribed to be devolved by the FC, the net proceeds should work out to Rs 238 [(100/42) x 100]. When this is applied to the actual figure of the taxes devolved and net proceeds are estimated, it falls short by net proceeds worked out by gross tax revenue – ((surcharges + cesses) + cost of collection) (Table 3.5). The discrepancy in net proceeds works out to Rs 8,83,170 crore during the period 2011-12 to 2018-19 BE.

Table 3.6: Components of Central resource transfer, 11th to 14th FC (till 2016-17)

FC	RD grants under Article 275 (Rs cr.)	Tax devolution (Rs cr.)	Central grants (Rs cr.)	RD grants/ Central grants (%)	RD grants + Tax devolution/ Central transfers (%)
11th	35,359	3,05,234	2,32,219	15.23	63.37
12th	56,856	6,91,785	5,60,718	10.14	59.77
13th	51,800	14,22,719	10,75,395	4.82	59.93
14th	90,214	11,14,054	6,81,987	13.23	67.05

Source: Budget documents of the Union and Reports of the Finance Commissions.

It also needs to be mentioned here that due to the lack of transparency in calculation of net proceeds (which is not published in the Union Budget documents), States are not in a position to understand the actual size of the divisible pool. It is relevant to point out here that the Comptroller and Auditor General (CAG) in Report 27 of 2016 (pp. 28-29) had observed as under:

> In terms of Article 279 of the Constitution, the Comptroller and Auditor General of India is required to ascertain and certify the 'net proceeds' (any tax or duty the proceeds thereof reduced by the cost of collection), whose certificate shall be final.
>
> During the certification of 'net proceeds' by the CAG, based on the recommendations of the successive Finance Commissions, it was noticed that during the period 1996-97 to 2014-15 an aggregated amount of Rs 81,647.70 crore was short devolved to the States.

The nonchalant attitude towards the CAG's observations to make computation of net proceeds more transparent is not only a disregard to the constitutional provisions but also exposes the lack of commitment to basic principles of cooperative federalism by successive central governments. The loss of share in taxes to the States on this account for the States works out to Rs 34,505 crore for the period 2011-12 to 2018-19 BE and on an average 2 per cent of the GDP at current prices. The cumulative loss of the States due to levy of surcharges and cesses and non-transparent computation of net proceeds is around 5 per cent of the GDP at current prices.

This loss to the States due to non-transparent accounting is nothing but a denial of resources from the divisible pool which is a constitutional right of the States. It is without factoring in these developments that the ToR of the 15th FC makes a mention of substantially enhanced devolution. This defies all logic and is contrary to facts.

As mentioned earlier, one other indicator of the pattern of transfers is the share of tied and untied grants in the resource flow to the States. All grants other than post-devolution revenue grants under Article 275 given on the basis of the recommendations of the FC are in the category of tied grants as States have only restricted degrees of freedom in utilizing them. There is a shift towards flexible resource flow from the Centre in the recommendations of the 14th FC which did away with sector specific grants and increased the tax share of the States, (though not to the full extent of what is apparent). But as can be seen from Table 3.6, the flexible component of central resource flow is stagnant and as a share of grants, and revenue deficit grants have substantially declined. The flexible part, however, shows an increase in the first two years of 14th FC recommendations. But the tenor of the ToR of the 15th FC stokes fears of a return to a context with a higher proportion of tied and performance-based grants. This would distort the overall budgetary position and adversely impact the expenditure priorities of the States by restricting their fiscal freedom and space.

The intrusion of the Centre into the fiscal territory of the States is clear from the increase in central spending on subjects in the State and Concurrent Lists. Chakraborty and Chakraborty (2018) have pointed out that the Union government's spending on subjects in the State List increased from 13 per cent of the revenue expenditure in

2002-03 to 23 per cent in 2008-09. Though it declined subsequently, it was as high as 16 per cent of revenue expenditure in 2015-16. The percentage of central revenue expenditure outlay on subjects in the Concurrent List increased from 11.8 per cent in 2002-03 to 16.4 per cent in 2015-16. This is because conditional grants have been used to enter into the spending domain of the States, with States having no say on the spending pattern or conditionalities associated with it. State budgets have to bear a fiscal cost on the programmes with rigid criteria fixed by the Centre. This goes against the economic rationale of the subsidiarity principle and increases the vertical imbalances between the Union and the States.

ABOLITION OF PLANNING COMMISSION AND ITS AFTERMATH

The Planning Commission which was a non-constitutional body, brought into being through an Executive Order in 1951, occupied an important place in formulating strategies of development in its initial years. Over the years, there were criticisms that it had become an alternative channel of grant disbursement parallel to the constitutional body, namely, the Finance Commission (Gulati and George 1988). The planning process was also viewed as one which is centralized and gave inadequate consideration to the States and the local governments. However, in so far as the fiscal side was concerned, States could formulate their plans and finalize their size after discussion with the Planning Commission. This prevented the accretion of absolute authority in the hands of the Union finance ministry on the aspect of borrowings by the States.

With the abolition of the Planning Commission since 2014, the States have lost even this limited leeway in an otherwise centralized framework. When considered in the general context of economic liberalization since 1991, the abolition of the Planning Commission seems to be the culmination of a process which was transforming it from an agency with the aim of formulating economic policies to one which was to oversee the process of privatization and lesser state intervention. The observation made by Patnaik (2014) cited below aptly summarizes this:

> It signifies the completion of a transition from a 'Nehruvian state', even a residual Nehruvian state that willy-nilly pursues neo-liberal policies rather than anything remotely resembling a Nehru-Mahalanobis strategy, to a full-fledged neo-liberal state. . . . Such a full-fledged neo-liberal state is characterised not just by a set of policies that fall under the rubric of neo-liberalism. It has a set of specific institutional features as well. These include: the 'autonomy' of the central bank; the elevation of the Ministry of Finance to the status of a super ministry dominating all others; . . .

With gross budgetary support (GBS) for State plans from the Centre no longer there, the fiscal burden of the States has increased and this is compounded by the unilateral announcement of national level programmes in the Union budget, which puts an additional fiscal burden on the States. One recent example is the National Health Protection Programme, Ayushman Bharat, in which the States are to share a part of the cost of implementation. This programme is ironically termed as an example of cooperative federalism, in which consensual decisions are to be taken. In the instant case, the States were not even consulted in the pre-announcement stage, even though they are to share a part of the cost.

CONTINUING ENCROACHMENT INTO STATES' SPENDING DOMAIN – RECENT EXPERIENCE

The Union Budget, 2018, announced a new scheme which is now nomenclatured as Pradhan Mantri Jan Arogya Yojana subsuming the present scheme of Rashtriya Swasthya Bima Yojana (RSBY). The scheme announced as a flagship scheme by the Centre would impact the States' finances in more ways than one. Chaudhary (2018) finds that

> if the State governments are required to foot 40 per cent of the cost of the scheme, the scheme would put a huge fiscal burden on many States. States which opt for the scheme will have to spend a substantial amount as a share of contribution towards this insurance scheme, leaving little room for any other health spending in States. The need for partial payment of premiums by States is likely to squeeze funds out of the public health system. Such an imposition would infringe upon the autonomy of the State Governments to independently design policies and programmes in the health sector, which is constitutionally in their domain.
>
> States that already have their own health insurance schemes will face other problems. In many such States, the population covered under the State schemes is larger than the BPL population identified by the Union Government while the sum assured is lower than the amount announced by the Finance Minister. Given this, there would be pressure on these States to upgrade their State-level schemes to match the benefits provided under the central government scheme. This would further add to the fiscal burden in such States.

The Kerala budget (2018) also takes note of the additional fiscal burden over and above the State's in the cost of the scheme:

> [I]n the central Budget presented yesterday a National Insurance Scheme of Rs. 5 lakh has been announced. In the pre-budget memorandum, Kerala had requested the central Government to enhance the benefits under RSBY. Along with welcoming the higher insurance benefits I share the apprehension of Kerala Government. It has been known that the eligibility of States with respect to 10 crore beneficiary families will be determined based on the socio-economic census. Consequently, a lion-share of families presently under RSBY in our State may get excluded from the insurance coverage. This is a major setback for the health sector in Kerala.
>
> . . . [E]ven while awaiting the details of the new scheme I would like to clarify the Comprehensive Health Programme of Kerala. All beneficiaries presently under RSBY scheme will be included in the new National Scheme even if the State Government has to remit the Insurance Premium. Anybody who [is] eligible but excluded from the present RSBY Scheme will also be included in the new scheme. In addition to this, people belonging to middle class and the rest will be encouraged to enrol in the scheme by remitting the entire premium on their own. It will be contemplated on how to connect Service Pension Scheme with this. Thus Kerala will become the first State in India that ensures Universal Health Security.

The scheme fails the test of adherence to the basic tenets of cooperative federalism and distorts the health expenditure priorities of the State. A more desirable scheme would have been improvising of existing State-level schemes taking into consideration region specific requirements with central assistance.

In conclusion, it can be stated that despite tall talk about cooperative federalism, in reality, the centralizing tendencies in the polity appear to have gathered momentum and with renewed vigour. Though cooperative federalism is the stated motto, the States' rights are being eroded in a much more substantial manner.

The National Development Council was an important forum where the State chief ministers could articulate their views and ventilate their grievances. This forum has become defunct after the planning process was done away with. Fiscally, the States lost an important source of formula-based grants that used to come in the form of Normal Central Assistance, known as Gadgil formula grants for the State plans.

In the Planning Commission era, the States also could discuss their borrowing limits during the annual plan discussions. Now the Union finance ministry is the sole authority in this regard. Though cooperative federalism recurs in the rhetoric, the Inter State Council, which has a constitutional mandate (Article 263), still remains dormant. NITI Aayog, which has taken the place of the Planning Commission is acting as a think tank of officials for the Union and has no effective role in either developing or changing policies for India. Added to these are the challenges on the revenue mobilization front faced by the States and the constraining of their fiscal space through the FRBM targets. It is these aspects we focus on in the following chapter.

CHAPTER 4

FISCAL RESPONSIBILITY AND BUDGET MANAGEMENT ACT: ITS IMPACT ON FISCAL SPACE

The FRBM Acts (of the Centre and the States) are essentially the neoliberal response to the fiscal crisis of the States in the latter part of the 1990s. The legislations in India were prompted by similar measures adopted in the United States of America (USA) and Europe. In the USA, the 'Gramm–Rudman–Hollings Act' of 1985 and 1987 was passed to control the fiscal deficit of the government, but has since been amended several times to permit larger borrowings. In the European Union, the 'Growth and Stability Pact' was adopted to enforce budgetary discipline in all countries using the Euro. Germany was the main mover behind the introduction of the pact. The irrationality of the pact was soon understood by Germany itself, when Germany and France went through a major economic recession in the early 2000s. For four years in succession since 2002, Germany broke the ceiling of 3 per cent set by the pact for budget deficits. '*It is only recently that targets have been realized in many countries, and even that based on suspect statistics.*'[1]As on 2005, 6 of the 12 Euro-area countries were facing procedural action under Article 104 of the EC Treaty for excessive deficits (Zeitler

[1] See http://ec.europa.eu/eurostat/documents/2995521/8824490/2-23042018-AP-EN.pdf/6e5b346e-e302-4132-920a-854b00ac196d.

2005). In 7 countries, the consolidated gross debt ratio in 2004 was above the 60 per cent reference value for debts (ibid.).

Despite the dubious theoretical foundations and the shaky international experience, the policy makers in India enthusiastically embraced the legislative route to fiscal consolidation. In this chapter, we discuss the salient features of the FRBM Acts in India, the experience with them so far and how they asymmetrically affected the State finances. We begin with a brief outline of the fiscal crisis of the 1990s. Our task is simple since in Chapters 2 and 3 we have already laid down the long-run trends in central and State finances.

FISCAL CRISIS IN THE 1990s

Though the roots of the crisis in State finances in India can be traced to the constitutional arrangement of Centre–State financial relations, the present deterioration had its origins in the mid-1980s, when the States as a whole started recording revenue deficits. As we saw in Chapter 2, the States had revenue surpluses on an average during the 1970s and early 1980s. The revenue deficit increased gradually between 1986-87 and 1997-98, and thereafter increased sharply till 1999-2000. Interestingly, the fiscal deficit of all States was rarely above 3 per cent till 1997-98. However, driven by the rise in the revenue deficit, the fiscal deficit of the States rose sharply after 1997-98 (Table 2.9). The two major factors that pushed the States into recording high revenue deficits during the second half of the 1990s were exogenous and generated by the central government policies, viz. a rise in interest rates and implementation of the Fifth Pay Commission's recommendations.

The latter half of the 1980s marked the end of the era of low and administered interest rates. Interest rates rose sharply thereafter, but as Chaudhuri (2000) has pointed out, its impact was masked by the presence of pre-existing cheap debt that the States had earlier availed of. From the latter half of the 1990s, the high cost debts incurred took their toll on the interest burden of the States and started a process of debt escalation. The earlier policy of the cancellation of part of States' debts by FCs had been given up by then. The severity of the imbalance in State finances in the1980s and 1990s has been the topic of many scholarly enquiries (Bagchi, Bajaj and Byrd 1992; Rao 1992; Kurian 1999; Chaudhuri 2000; Vithal and Sastry 2001; Rao 2002; EPWRF 2004).

The role of the central government was critical in the process of deterioration of State finances. The rates of interest on borrowing by States increased sharply after the mid-1980s, and especially after 1990-91. The coupon rates of State government securities were raised sharply by the RBI from 1990-91 onwards. The weighted average of coupon rates, which was 11.5 per cent in 1990-91, reached its historic peak of 14 per cent in 1995-96. In the same period, the interest rates on small savings borrowings by the States also increased from 13 per cent in 1990-91 to 14.5 per cent in 1992-93, and remained stable till 1997-98.

These rates of interest that the States had to pay were clearly usurious, much higher than the growth rate of the GDP and thus, a sure recipe for fiscal disaster. Even though the interest rates started falling thereafter, the financial burden that these high rates of interest placed on State finances was significant. The interest payments of States increased from Rs 8,655 crore in 1990-91 to Rs 21,932 crore in 1995-96 and Rs 62,489 crore in 2001-02. As a percentage of total revenue receipts, these interest payments amounted to 13 per cent in 1990-91, 16 per cent in 1995-96 and 24 per cent in 2001-02.

In the period during which the Centre was raising the rates of interest on States' borrowings, the rates of interest on the Centre's borrowings were not only at lower levels, but were also rising at a much slower rate. The result was that the differential between the rates of interest borne by the Centre and the States widened significantly during the 1990s, which continued into the 2000s (Chandrasekhar and Ghosh 2005a; EPWRF 2004). In fact, the differential in every year in the early 2000s was higher than the same for any year during the period 1980-2000. The average rate of interest of States' borrowings was above 10 per cent even in 2004, while that of the Centre had dipped below 7 per cent.

In 1997-98, there was another shock to State finances, when the recommendations of the Fifth Pay Commission were implemented. This measure sharply raised the levels of the revenue deficit recorded by States from 1997-98 onwards. In just one year, the revenue deficit of states more than doubled – from 1.1 per cent in 1997-98 to 2.5 per cent in 1998-99. While we do not wish to neglect other factors, the rise in the interest burden and higher salary commitment constituted the two most prominent factors responsible for the deterioration of State finances. The outcome of these two factors was a sharp rise in the debt burden of the States. As a percentage of GDP, the total debt outstanding of the States increased from 21 per cent in March 1997 to 26.1 per cent in March 2000 and 33.1 per cent in March 2006.

To compound the above two factors that contributed to the escalation in expenditure, on the revenue side there were visible signs of slowdown. The own tax revenue to GDP ratio of the Centre as well as buoyancy of central taxes fell during the 1990s (Table 2.3) as a result of substantial reductions of tax rates, both in direct and indirect taxes, and these reductions failing to raise tax compliance levels. The own tax revenue of the States also fell during this period, as a result of tax competition indulged in by the States to attract big private investments. This slowdown in the revenue side and rising expenditure commitments were the main reasons for rising deficits at the central and State levels. Added to these, the growth of the economy also slowed down. As already seen in previous chapters, the ratio of central transfers to GDP fell during the 1990s (Table 3.1) which further exacerbated the fiscal downturn in the States.

INTRODUCTION OF THE FRBM ACT

It was in this context that the FRBM Bill was introduced in Parliament in 2000. The task force appointed by the Government on the FRBM Act noted that 'The gravity of the situation, and the multi-year process of debate and discussion, led to a far-sighted response. All political parties voted in favour of the Fiscal Responsibility and Budgetary Management Act 2003. It is the deeply held view of the task force that their implementation will reshape our destiny, and take India to a commanding position in the world economy' (GoI 2004, p. 13).

It was thus firmly believed in neoliberal circles, as exemplified by the report of the task force, that 'there is an innate synergy between acceleration of GDP growth and fiscal consolidation' (ibid.). As the first step, the government appointed the E.A.S. Sarma Committee to prepare a draft of the legislation; this committee submitted its report in July 2000. The FRBM Act was passed by the Lok Sabha on May 7, 2003, and by the Rajya Sabha on July 29, 2003. The Bill was passed by a voice vote, and not unanimously, as the task force had erroneously claimed. Members from the Left parties had raised their serious objections to the provisions in the Bill (*People's Democracy*, August 10, 2003). The Bill was notified as an Act on August 26, 2003.

In this version of the Act, the government had to eliminate the revenue deficit by 2005-06. In July 2004, the Act was amended to postpone the year of elimination of revenue deficit to 2008-09. In February 2004, a task force was appointed by the government to 'draw up the medium term framework for fiscal policies to achieve the FRBM objectives', and 'also formulate the annual targets indicating the path of adjustment and required policy measures' (GoI 2004, p. 201). Introducing its projections on fiscal consolidation, the task force noted that 'States finances would obtain an enormous boost under the proposals of this report' (ibid.).

Concurrently, the Centre was also forcing the hands of the States to pass similar Acts in their legislative assemblies. The FCs chose to have a narrow definition of 'constitutional transfers' to mean only the divisible pool. The other grants and benefits were held to be over and above the 'constitutional transfers' and thus could be tied to specific conditions. For the first time, the 11th FC started the process of linking resource transfers and other benefits from the Centre to fiscal consolidation by the States. The passage of the FRBM Acts at the State level became an indicator of the progress achieved by States in fiscal consolidation. States were asked to model their legislations on the legislation prepared by the Centre. Karnataka was the first to pass an FRBM Act in August 2002. Kerala, Tamil Nadu and Punjab followed suit in 2003. Uttar Pradesh passed its legislation in 2004. The other State governments, with the exception of a few, passed their FRBM Acts in 2005 and 2006. As on August 2006, 23 states had passed FRBM Acts (Ministry of Finance 2006). The hurried passage of these legislations in 2005 and 2006 by many states was the consequence of the conditionalities put forward by the 12th FC. States had to pass the FRBM Act in 2005 itself to take advantage of the debt rescheduling scheme offered by the 12th FC. The main elements of the FRBM Acts passed by the States were the following:

a) 3 per cent target for fiscal deficit to be achieved by 2005-06 to 2010-11;
b) elimination of revenue deficit by around the same time;
c) limits to state government guarantees on debt;
d) limits to overall liabilities that could be incurred;
e) formulation of a medium-term fiscal plan to reach these targets; and
f) institution of a complaint redressal mechanism.

The surprising rapidity with which FRBM Acts were passed by

the States is an issue that requires some examination by political scientists. The United Democratic Front (UDF) government in Kerala, in a fit of reform fury, set a 2 per cent ceiling for the fiscal deficit by 2006-07. This was later amended, but the fact that any political leadership could even propose a 2 per cent ceiling for the fiscal deficit is indeed intriguing. The key players in this process were the bureaucracies of the State governments, who had totally internalized the neoliberal reform rhetoric. How else could one explain the proposal of a 2 per cent ceiling for the fiscal deficit?

ROLE OF THE FINANCE COMMISSIONS

The Constitution has defined the role of the FCs to be one of making recommendations on 'the distribution between the Union and the States of the net proceeds of taxes' and setting 'principles which should govern the grants-in-aid of the revenues of the states out of the Consolidated Fund of India'. In other words, the FCs were supposed to act as a neutral arbitrator to fix the levels of transfer of resources from the Centre to States as well as the distribution of these transferred resources across States.

However, in recent years, extra-constitutional powers have been given to the FCs through the specification of additional ToR by the central government. These powers have been provided to the FCs in order to make their reports correspond to the policies being advocated by the central government. For instance, the ToR of the 11th FC included the mandate to 'draw a monitorable fiscal reforms programme aimed at reduction of revenue deficit of the States and recommend the manner in which grants to States . . . may be linked to progress in implementing this programme'. In fact, under Article 275 of the Constitution, the FCs have no powers to impose conditionalities on resource transfers to States in the form of statutory grants assessed on the basis of needs of each State.

All the recent FCs have been given the mandate to review the finances of the central and State governments, and suggest measures to maintain the path of 'sound' fiscal consolidation, through their terms of reference. The 14th FC recommended the target fiscal deficit of 3 per cent of the GSDP for all the States. States were allowed a borrowing flexibility of 0.50 per cent provided they did not run a revenue deficit in the year in which borrowing limits were to be fixed and the immediately preceding year. The 13th FC had also previously recommended a 3 per cent fiscal deficit target for the Centre and the States. It had further set a combined target of 68 per cent debt to GDP for the Centre and States. The Commission also extended the benefit of Debt Consolidation and Relief Facility (DCRF)[2] to Sikkim and West Bengal on the condition that they adopt a fiscal responsibility legislation.

There had been a number of criticisms (including the dissent note to its report by one of the members, Amaresh Bagchi) of the 11th FC exceeding its constitutional brief in proposing conditionalities on central transfers. The 12th FC had ToR similar to the 11th FC, including the mandate to 'review the state of the finances of the Union and the States and suggest a plan by which the governments, collectively and severally, may bring about a restructuring of the public finances [by] restoring budgetary balance [and] achieving macroeconomic stability and debt reduction along with equitable growth'. The 12th FC was also given powers to 'review the Fiscal

[2] The 12th FC recommended the Debt Consolidation and Relief Facility (DCRF), which involved the consolidation of central loans (excluding loans given for Centrally Sponsored Schemes (CSS)/Central Plan schemes through ministries other than the Ministry of Finance) to the States contracted till March 2004 and outstanding on March 31, 2005, and rescheduling them for a fresh term of twenty years, resetting the interest rate to be charged on them at 7.5 per cent along with a debt write-off. An individual State could avail of the DCRF only if it enacted a fiscal responsibility legislation prescribing specific annual deficit reduction targets in order to ultimately eliminate the revenue deficit by 2008-09 and reduce the fiscal deficit to 3 per cent of Gross State Domestic Product (GSDP).

Reform Facility introduced by the central Government on the basis of the recommendations of the 11th FC, and suggest measures for effective achievement of its objectives'.

The 12th FC recommended a fiscal restructuring plan in its report, according to which a) the revenue deficit had to be eliminated by 2008-09; b) the fiscal deficit had to be brought down to 3 per cent in 2008-09; and c) annual targets were set for the reduction of the revenue and fiscal deficits (0.4 percentage points for the revenue deficit and 0.3 percentage points for the fiscal deficit for all States put together). Each State had to enact a fiscal responsibility legislation to this effect. The 12th FC, in order to address the rising debt burden of the States, also recommended a general scheme of debt relief and a loan write-off scheme. As per the general scheme, all loans from the Centre (excluding the high-cost loans under NSSF) were to be consolidated and a uniform interest of 7.5 per cent charged on them. Under the loan write-off scheme, repayments on loans from the Centre between 2005-06 and 2009-10 were to be written-off, with the quantum of write-off linked to the absolute amount of reduction of revenue deficit of the State in each successive year as well as the containment of the fiscal deficit at the level of 2004-05. The benefits of both these schemes were to be made available to only those States that had passed FRBM legislations.

Such had been the environment generated by the neoliberal reformers that few States were not willing to break the rules. Only the West Bengal government had refused to pass an FRBM Act. State governments on the whole had been moving fast to meet the targets set by FRBM Acts and the 12th FC. The revenue deficit for all States had declined from 2.9 per cent of the GDP in 1999-2000 to 0.7 per cent of the GDP in 2005-06.

CRITIQUE OF THE FRBM ACT

The theoretical underpinning of the FRBM Act is the pre-Keynesian British Treasury view, which considered public debt as something akin to private borrowings and budgets were to be balanced every year. The growth enhancing impact of public debt was never considered and this view had been subjected to sharp criticism years back by Domar (1944). The deficits of the government were seen as crowding out private investments, while the crowding in effects of public investment were ignored. Since the 1940s, this view had become a past relic. The Treasury view was set aside by the Keynesian revolution. But the failure of the Keynesian policies and stagflation of 1973 led to the resurrection of the fiscal conservatism as reflected in the FRBM targets. The numerical targets of 3 per cent fiscal deficit and 60 per cent debt to GDP ratio have neither theoretical nor empirical substantiation. Economists from the left have been the most consistent and vocal critics of the central policies of framing legislations to cap revenue and fiscal deficits (Patnaik 2000, 2001; Chandrasekhar and Ghosh 2000, 2001, 2005a, b).

Besides, the strident dissent from the left economists, even the erstwhile Planning Commission in its Approach Paper to the 11th Five-Year Plan, was compelled to critically view the implications of continuing with the FRBM Acts for any strategy of development that would require acceleration of revenue expenditure. It also discussed the issue of fiscal deficit targets in the FRBM Acts. It stated that important plan expenditures, such as in infrastructure, might have to be postponed if the targets of fiscal deficit were adhered to. Such postponement, the paper argues, 'could jeopardize growth' and reduce the space available for 'counter-cyclical fiscal measures' in times of economic slowdown. The Planning Commission, in its attempt to have 'faster' but 'more inclusive' growth in the 11th Five-

Year Plan, had outlined a strategy that included a number of new initiatives such as the expansion of school education, programmes for provision of health care, drinking water, rural infrastructure and schemes for 'bridging the divides'. All those ambitious programmes belonged essentially to the development revenue expenditure category and could not be implemented if the FRBM and 12th FC targets of elimination of revenue deficit were to be adhered to.

Furthermore, it is important to accept that a one-size-fits-all approach in case of deficit targeting is inherently flawed given the highly diverse conditions prevailing in the States of India. Backward States like Bihar, Uttar Pradesh or Rajasthan, with absence of quality infrastructure, have huge capital expenditures to undertake. For such States, running high revenue deficits is not advisable, as it compresses the space available for capital expenditure. However, for middle income States like Kerala and Tamil Nadu, the compulsion of zero revenue deficit makes little sense, as the funds requirement for maintaining the already existing infrastructure is substantial. FRBM restrictions which do not factor in such differences create needless hurdles.

More recently, the Union government has started feeling the need to bend the fiscal targets under the FRBM Act. Faced with a slowing economy and an urgency to increase spending, many government functionaries, most notably the erstwhile Chief Economic Advisor Arvind Subramanian, have questioned the rationale of an arbitrarily set 3 per cent fiscal deficit target (dissent note to the FRBM Review Committee Report, 2017), on the argument that it unnecessarily restricts government spending at a time when such spending is needed, and when the government clearly has the capacity to comfortably service its debt.

Across countries, the pause button on deficit targets had to be pushed in the wake of the global economic crisis and governments were forced to resurrect the Keynesian prescriptions

Table 4.1: WMA from RBI as a source for financing States, as a ratio of total liabilities, 1980-81 to 2016-17 (%)

Period	WMA as a ratio of total liabilities (%)
1980-81 to 1989-90	1.71
1990-91 to 1999-2000	0.78
2000-01 to 2009-10	0.30
2010-11to 2016-17	0.05

Source: *Handbook of Statistics on Indian Economy*, various issues.

of expansionary fiscal policies and India too had been part of this. Had fiscal conservatism been adhered to, the consequences would have been chaotic. Though there is a rollback, it is not to the pre-crisis levels.

ASYMMETRIC IMPACT OF FRBM ON THE UNION AND STATES

The impact of the FRBM guidelines on Union and State governments is asymmetric, due to the simple fact that the Centre can postpone the achievement of targets, or modify the central FRBM Act to move forward the targets set. As we have seen in Chapter 2, during the period 2010-11 to 2016-17, the average fiscal deficit of the States to GDP was only 2.48 per cent, while that of the central government was 3.16 per cent. In 2017-18, the Centre's fiscal deficit to GDP ratio, even after window dressing by including GST cess, States' share in IGST as Centre's revenue and by forcing cash surplus ONGC to foot the bill of disinvestment of HPCL Ltd, taking disinvestment proceeds to Rs 91,257 core,[3] was at 3.5 per cent of GDP. Even for the current year, 2018-19 the budget estimate is 3.2 per cent.

On the contrary, the State governments would have no option but to postpone capital investments or important social sector spending in case of an inability to meet the targets. This has had a

[3] See Receipts Budget 2018 of the Union at finmin.nic.in.

Figure 4.1: WMA – Total liabilities ratio of States, 1980-81 to 2016-17 (%)

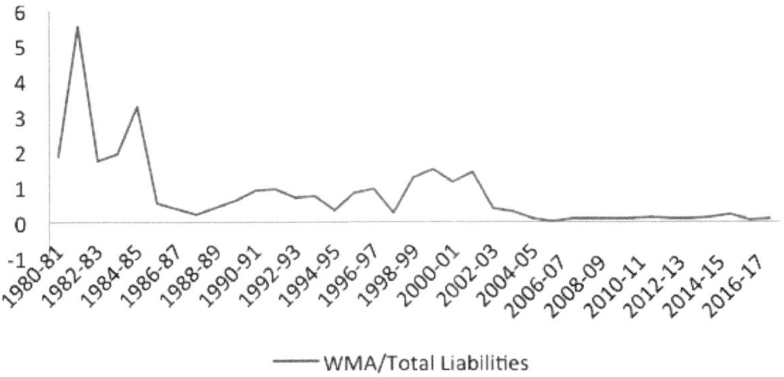

Source: *Handbook of Statistics on Indian Economy*, RBI, various issues.

perverse consequence of a permanent situation of cash surplus in the treasuries of the State governments.

When State governments' day-to-day disbursement requirements are in excess of receipts, temporary accommodation is sought from the RBI in the form of Ways and Means Advances (WMA). Ceilings have been determined for each State and when the WMA exceeds the ceiling, the State incurs an overdraft (OD). The persistence of an OD beyond a specified period would result in temporary suspension of treasury operations by the RBI. State finances in India, from the latter half of the 1980s, were distinctly characterized by the persistence of cash balance deficits and consequent availing of WMA and OD from RBI. However, since the early 2000s, the situation underwent a change and the extent to which State governments availed of WMA from the RBI declined sharply.

As Table 4.1 shows, the WMA as a source of financing States' liquidity problems has become almost non-existent. It rose during the period 1998-99 to 2000-01. Subsequently, it fell and reached nil or negligible levels during the period 2005-06 to 2016-17 (Figure

Table 4.2: Availing of WMA by States, 2006-07 to 2013-14

WMA	2006-07	2007-08	2008-09	2009-10	2010-11	2011-12	2012-13	2013-14
Non-special category States								
0-99	2	1	4	5	2	3	3	4
100-199	Nil	2	Nil	1	2	1	1	Nil
200 and above	1	Nil	Nil	Nil	Nil	Nil	Nil	Nil
Special category States								
0-99	5	4	2	3	2	3	2	4
100-199	Nil	Nil	Nil	Nil	Nil	1	2	Nil
200 and above	Nil	Nil	Nil	Nil	Nil	Nil	Nil	Nil

Source: *RBI Annual Report*, various issues.

Note: Comparable data are not published since 2013-14.

Table 4.3: Cash surplus of all States, 2000-01 to 2017-18 (Rs crore)

Year	Cash surplus invested in 14-day treasury bills (outstanding in March)
2000-01	100
2001-02	543
2002-03	3,099
2003-04	3,379
2004-05	14,344
2005-06	53,351
2006-07	59,236
2007-08	68,942
2008-09	1,14,539
2009-10	1,07,129
2010-11	1,15,450
2011-12	1,17,180
2012-13	1,42,220
2013-14	1,10,180
2014-15	1,09,080
2015-16	1,22,490
2016-17	1,56,060
2017-18	1,50,870

Source: *Weekly Statistical Supplement*, RBI, and *RBI Bulletin*, various issues.

Figure 4.2: Cash Surplus of States, 2000-01 to 2017-18 (Rs crore)

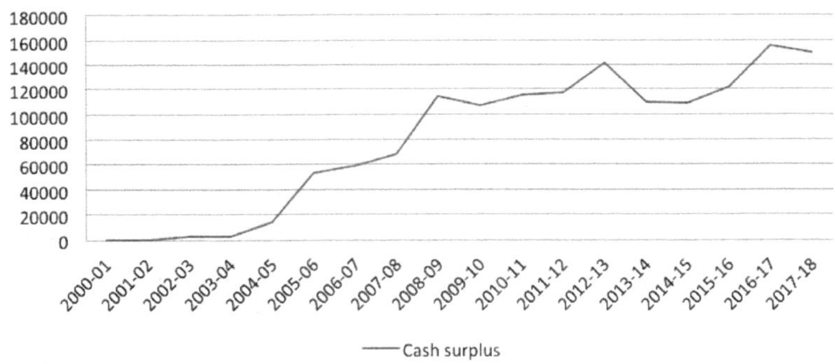

Source: *Weekly Statistical Supplement*, RBI, and *RBI Bulletin*, various issues.

4.1). The number of non-special category States that availed of normal WMA for 200 days or more declined from 14 to just one between 2000-01 and 2005-06. Out of the 17 states, 13 were not in WMA for even a day in 2005-06 (SAAC and Ramakumar 2006).

This trend has continued from 2006-07 as can be seen from Table 4.2.

It can be seen that not more than 4 States out of 28 have availed of WMA facility in any year since 2006-07 to 2013-14 and no State has availed of WMA for more than 200 days since 2007-08 till 2013-14.

The contrary phenomenon of surplus in cash balances, which was a relatively rare phenomenon in the 1990s, began to be a regular feature of the States' treasuries in the 2000s. As on March 31, 2018, the treasury cash balance of States is at Rs 1,50,870 crore as against Rs 53,351 crore as on March 31, 2006 (Table 4.3). When there is a surplus balance in the treasury, the RBI invests the surplus in the 14-day intermediate treasury bills of the central government on behalf of the States. In effect, it results in investment of amounts borrowed by States at interest rates ranging from 7 to 8.5 per cent getting invested in 14-day intermediate treasury bills issued by the Centre earning an interest rate of 4.5 to 5 per cent interest.

This is a case of cheap ways and means for the Centre at the cost of States, accentuating the already existing fiscal asymmetry. It can be seen from Table 4.3 that the cash surplus invested in the 14-day treasury bills increased rapidly to Rs 1.14 lakh crores in 2008-09. Since then, till 2014-15, it hovered around that level, except during 2012-13 when it rose to Rs 1.42 lakh crore. Only during 2009-10, 2013-14 and 2014-15, has there been an absolute decline when compared with the previous year. But since 2016-17, it has once more resumed a marked upward trend and is currently around Rs 1.5 lakh crores (Table 4.3 and Figure 4.2). The Reserve Bank of India views this as inefficient cash management by the State governments (RBI 2018, p. 19). But the fact that the basic reason driving the rise in cash surpluses is the FRBM mandated deficit target imposed through FC awards, which hamstring the States from spending borrowed funds, is conveniently left unmentioned.

The phenomenon of significant investment by States in treasury bills is worrisome for a number of reasons. First, as already stated the investments by States in the 14-day intermediate treasury bills of the Centre earn them a return of 5 per cent per annum. However, as we shall see, the average cost of mobilization of funds for the States is much higher. In 2005-06, the interest rate on borrowings of States against small savings was 9.5 per cent per annum (the costliest debt in the market) and the average interest rate on market borrowings was 7.4 per cent per annum. The total transfer of NSSF loans from the Centre to the States was Rs 90,000 crore in 2005-06. At the end of the same period, the total reverse investment by States in the treasury bills was Rs 53,351 crore, or about two-thirds of its NSSF borrowing! Even the RBI, in a study on State finances, commented that this situation implies a 'reverse transfer of resources from States to the Centre' (RBI 2005a, p. 52).

Secondly, the Centre has also been recycling the cash surplus of States to itself at a very low rate of interest for treasury security operations. In 2005-06, the Centre enjoyed a surplus cash balance for most months of the year. According to the RBI, 'had it not been for the investments of States' surplus cash balances in 14-day intermediate treasury bills, the Centre would have been in WMA' in 2005-06 (ibid.). Also, the Centre deploys its cash balances in securities held by the RBI (which fetches the Centre a yield higher than 5 per cent), thus saving on the interest to be paid on the dated securities held by the RBI (ibid.). This has enabled the Centre to make profits, through positive spreads, from the States' cash surpluses. There was a growing resentment among States against this reverse flow of resources. Many States have openly stated that they do not want to borrow from the NSSF. As a result, NSSF borrowings have been almost phased out since the recommendations of the 14th FC. Still, the issue of mounting cash surplus persists. One is amazed at the total absence of discussions on how the surplus cash balances can be fruitfully employed to meet the basic needs of the people. There is a peculiar myopia towards the expenditure side of the problem.

Then why do the States not spend this money? The then Union finance minister while trying to explain this phenomenon in Parliament during 2006-07 budget discussions put the blame on the States, for not addressing the spending needs in education, health care, the mid-day meal scheme, rural roads and urban development. The problem, according to him, is that states are 'unable to spend' because they do not have the 'absorptive capacity'. Nothing can be farther from the truth (Isaac and Ramakumar 2006).

States do not spend because there are legal constraints on spending. The finance ministry and the successive Union FCs have forced the States to pass FRBM legislations in their assemblies. As per these, States have to eliminate the revenue deficit and reduce the fiscal deficit to 3 per cent of the GSDP by 2008-09. In line with these targets, the revenue deficit and fiscal deficit of states declined sharply in the 2000s. This decline in revenue deficit was achieved by keeping the revenue expenditure to GDP ratio stagnant, even while there was an increase in revenue receipts to GDP ratio of states. The States could have raised revenue expenditures by making use of the increased receipts, and still kept the revenue deficit constant. This, however, would have been contrary to the targets set for the elimination of revenue deficit by 2008-09. Even the increased capital receipts in the form of NSSF borrowings were not routed to revenue expenditures because of the fear of rising revenue deficit. The cash surplus phenomenon, thus, is a perverse outcome of the FRBM Acts.

FRBM REVIEW COMMITTEE REPORT

The States have expressed their misgivings regarding the highly conservative targets of the FRBM Act, which are imposed upon them through the FCs. Even the Union government has had to miss its fiscal deficit targets in the wake of high spending requirements. Thus, in this backdrop, the government constituted the FRBM Review Committee under N.K. Singh, which submitted its report in January 2017. The committee has proposed that the FRBM Act, 2003 be replaced with the Debt Management and Fiscal Responsibility Bill, a draft of which has been prepared. In the Bill, the committee recommends the use of the debt to GDP ratio as the primary target for fiscal consolidation. It suggests a ceiling of 60 per cent debt to GDP ratio for Centre and the States, with 40 per cent limit for the Centre and 20 per cent for State governments. The draft Bill further proposes the fiscal deficit targets at 2.5 and 1.7 per cent respectively of the GDP for the Centre and the States, to be achieved by 2023. In the event of a national calamity, national security issue or other exceptional circumstances, an escape clause also allows for a deviation from the fiscal targets.

It is noteworthy that there has been criticism of many recommendations of the review committee by one of its members, Arvind Subramanian, the then Chief Economic Advisor to the Government of India. His contention is regarding the arbitrary nature of the guideline targets for the debt to GDP ratio set at 60 per cent and the fiscal and revenue deficit targets at 2.5 and 0.8 per cent of GDP respectively. The dissent note also observes that multiple targets force policy makers to aim at too many, and run the risk of not achieving any of the goals.

The deviation clause is also a point of disapproval. The condition that it can only be activated in case of a 3 percentage point fall in the GDP growth rate is whimsical, for at least two reasons. One,

Table 4.4: Deficit and debt indicators of Centre and States as percentage of GDP, 2000-01 to 2016-17

	2000-01	2005-06	2010-11	2011-12	2012-13	2013-14	2014-15	2015-16	2016-17
Revenue Deficit									
Combined	6.45	2.70	3.20	4.24	3.46	3.27	3.31	2.51	2.40
Centre	3.91	2.51	3.24	4.51	3.66	3.18	2.94	2.51	2.10
States	2.54	0.19	-0.04	-0.27	-0.20	0.09	0.37	0.00	0.30
Fiscal Deficit									
Combined	9.50	6.40	6.87	7.84	6.90	6.69	6.73	6.99	7.02
Centre	5.46	3.96	4.80	5.91	4.93	4.48	4.10	3.89	3.52
States	4.04	2.44	2.07	1.93	1.97	2.21	2.63	3.10	3.5
Borrowings & Liabilities									
Combined	87.01	95.41	75.65	76.28	74.78	74.16	73.25	75.40	74.20
Centre	59.36	63.90	52.15	53.46	52.55	52.16	51.52	51.88	50.30
States	27.65	31.51	23.50	22.82	22.33	22.00	21.73	23.52	23.90

Source: *Handbook of Statistics on Indian Economy*, RBI; *State Finances: A Study of the Budgets*, RBI, various issues; Budget documents of the Union.

by setting a cut-off GDP growth decline, it substantially limits the government's capacity to identify and avert a severe economic slowdown before it becomes deep. Two, it is important to recognize that a GDP growth rate fall from 8 per cent to 5 per cent is not the same as a fall from 6 per cent to 3 per cent. The latter case, especially in India, calls for an expansionary intervention much earlier that the one proposed under the Bill.

Besides, the logic and reasoning provided for a 60 per cent debt to GDP ratio target does not seem unimpeachable. The committee's report relies on studies by Reinhart and Rogoff (2008; 2010) that a 90 per cent debt ratio is sustainable for advanced countries and 60 per cent for Emerging Market Economies (EMEs) with a substantial external debt component. India would not fall in the latter category. The external debt as a proportion of total borrowings and liabilities is declining and is not substantial (Table 2.10). Given this, targeting a 60 per cent debt to GDP ratio as sustainable in the Indian context is not sound. The FRBM Review Committee has suggested a drastic cut in fiscal deficits of States from 3 to 1.7 per cent by 2022-23, in order to achieve this debt target which itself is not based on a correct appreciation of the country's fiscal situation.

IS MACROECONOMIC STABILITY STATES' RESPONSIBILITY?

As already stated, the FRBM Act, and the proposed Bill by the FRBM Review Committee emphasize on achieving fiscal and revenue deficit and debt targets. The trends of all these measures are presented in Table 4.4, for both the Union and State governments.

A look at the figures reveals that the fiscal situation continues to be asymmetric and particularly challenging for the Union government. The consolidated fiscal deficit of the Union and the State governments in 2016-17 was estimated at 7.02 per cent of GDP and the revenue deficit at 2.40 per cent of GDP, implying that a large proportion of borrowing is used to finance revenue expenditures due to the revenue deficit of 2.10 per cent of GDP for the Union government. It is also clear that although the States have mostly met their target of zero revenue deficit since the implementation of the FRBM Act in 2003, it is the Centre that has been responsible for almost the entire revenue deficit. The data also suggest that outstanding liabilities of both the central and the State governments have mostly stagnated around the 50-52 and 22-23 per cent levels, respectively. However, it should be noted that as per the draft Bill of the FRBM Review Committee, States should limit their debt to GDP ratio at 20 per cent whereas the Centre should restrict its at 40 per cent. It is evident from Table 4.4 above that the States are in a much better position as their debt has averaged around 22 per cent of the GDP while that of the Centre stood at around 50 per cent of the GDP.

The above data also suggest that in the recent years, the fiscal deficit and debt to GDP ratio has shown a steady decline, which is attributable to both the Centre and the States. However, the persistence of revenue deficit is almost fully attributable to the Centre in the last decade. It is quite apparent that the States have done their part, but more needs to be done on the part of the central government in this regard.

Given these facts and circumstances, the added asymmetry in fiscal deficit targets as a consequence of FRBM Review Committee recommendations does not auger well for the States, more so when the Union government has accepted the recommendations. It is in this context that the ToR of the 15th FC raises genuine apprehensions on the part of the States, especially as regards restrictions to be imposed on debt and deficits of the States. This would burden and constrain the fiscal space of the States and their intervention capacity in social and physical infrastructure sectors.

When demands for more flexibility are also fully endorsed by international experiences with fiscal responsibility legislations, the report of the FRBM Review Committee and the ToR of the 15th FC amount to accelerated movement in reverse gear. This is ominous for the States as well as for the economy as a whole. As we have argued, the FRBM Acts have to go off the rule book or need to be drastically amended. It is in this context that we discuss in the next chapter another recent constraint on the revenue side for the States, which are asymmetries and problems arising out of the GST regime and its implementation.

CHAPTER 5

POST-GST SCENARIO: STATES' REVENUE STRAITJACKETED

PRE-GST REGIME

In the initial constitutional division of powers, personal income tax, corporation tax (since 1957), excise (other than on alcoholic liquor for human consumption) and customs duties were in the domain of the Centre and taxes on intra-purchase and sale of goods was with the respective States. Taxing of services was not envisaged at that time. Service tax was brought in as a Union tax through the Finance Act, 1994, bringing a small number of services into the tax net, invoking the Residuary power in the Constitution, which is vested with the Centre. Gradually, this was widened and all services, except those in the negative list, were subject to service tax and service tax became one of the buoyant components of central taxes.

The States were taxing purchase and sale of goods within their territorial jurisdiction by the General Sales Tax, which was levied at the first point of sale within the State. There was also practice of multiple point of sale taxes on some commodities. Over and above this, turnover tax and surcharges were also levied in the case of many goods. Inter-State sales were subject to levy of Central Sales

Tax (CST),[1] a central tax, which was, however, levied and collected by the State in which the transaction originated. These multiple taxes and numerous rates of General Sales Tax, came in for much criticism for being a very complicated tax maze.

Further, there was the serious issue of the cascading effects of the indirect tax structure. Sales tax was levied on commodities that had been subjected to excise duty (and at times additional excise duty) levies and CST in the case of inter-State sales, besides various types of entry taxes. The resulting cascading burden of taxes was seen as having a range of extraneous adverse effects, including that of reducing the competitiveness of Indian exports. There was also a view that the sales tax structure had led to loss of tax buoyancy. It was entirely perceived as an officer centred tax system with attendant dangers of corruption and inefficiency. A response to leakage was the spread of the multi-point sales tax system so that it could be identified at one of the points by following the trail. The multi-point sales tax made the system even more cumbersome.

In the post-economic reforms period starting since the1990s, another issue cropped up as regards State taxation. The dismantling of the licensing system threw the field open for private capital and the States began to offer competitive tax holidays to attract big private investment. This was described as a 'fiscal race to the bottom' by multilateral financial institutions like the World Bank (Rao and Rao 2005). Floor rates below which sales tax rates should not be reduced were suggested. Origin-based taxes like CST were sought to be phased out as they were considered distortionary.

In view of these trends and the slowdown in growth of own tax revenues of the States, the General Sales Tax was sought to be replaced by Value Added Tax (VAT) for intra-State trade of goods with input tax credit for removing the cascading effect. The CST rate was gradually reduced from 4 per cent to 2 per cent with the aim

[1] This was introduced by the Sixth Constitution amendment in 1956.

of phasing it out. Uniform tax rates were introduced for intra-State sale of goods with input credit. VAT was introduced on April 1, 2005. The initial rates were 1, 4 and 12.5 per cent respectively which were subsequently raised to 2, 5 and 14.5 per cent respectively.

This standardization of rates was, however, done through consensual decisions of the Empowered Committee of State Finance Ministers. But this measure came in for criticism on the ground that there was persuasion on the States to surrender their constitutional right to fix tax rates in spirit, though it remained in letter. It was opined that in a vast country with diverse tastes and preferences, having uniform tax rates would not be a desirable tax reform. Moreover, lower tax rates under the new VAT regime and the necessity to give input tax credit was seen as leading to revenue loss for the States. However, VAT was implemented since April 1, 2005, by most of the States, though some States, namely, Tamil Nadu and Uttar Pradesh implemented it later.

Experience reveals that VAT revenues were buoyant till 2012-13 as the new self-policing system mopped up the slack that existed in the tax system. However, after 2012-13 there was a decline in the growth rates of tax revenue. A major blow to the VAT system was the verdict of the Supreme Court on levy of entry tax. The VAT tax was an intra-State tax and therefore without the entry tax there was no possibility of taxing commodities that were brought from outside States ostensibly for own use. This was particularly the case of a consumer State like Kerala. There was a substantial reduction in the growth rate of revenues under VAT in many States from an average of 16-18 per cent from 2005-06 to 2012-13 to 8-10 per cent per annum starting 2013-14. Expenditure burdens of the States, especially in the revenue account were downwardly inflexible. This prompted States to look for expanding their tax base.

EMERGENCE OF GST

Under the circumstances narrated above, adding the services sector, which comprised about 60 per cent or more of the GDP, to the States' tax base and levying consumption taxes on destination basis seemed attractive to many States, especially the States with a smaller production and manufacturing base. These two positive expectations of major gains made most of the States welcome implementation of the Goods and Services Tax (GST), which taxed supply of goods and services. Central taxes like excise duty, service tax and State VAT and CST were subsumed in GST since its implementation on July 1, 2017. States added the service sector to their tax base and the Centre could tax upto the retail sales stage as against only upto the manufacturing stage under the central excise regime.

However, under GST, a uniform national tax rate would prevail and States would have to surrender their right to determine rates. But this was a right that was already surrendered to the Empowered Committee of Finance Ministers who oversaw the implementation of VAT. What was de facto lost was only going to be lost de jure. The uniformity of tax rates which was suggested and implemented on the basis of recommendations of the non-statutory Empowered Committee of State Finance Ministers (hereafter Empowered Committee) during the VAT regime is now done by a Council of Union and State Finance Ministers, comprising the GST Council constituted under Article 279A of the Constitution inserted by the 101st Constitution amendment.

The implication of GST for States' autonomy in taxation was an issue that was elaborately discussed in the Empowered Committee. A major decision was the rejection of the suggestion that a single tax be collected by a single authority and then apportioned between the Centre and the States. The Indian GST was to be jointly administered by the Centre and States with the Centre collecting Central GST (CGST) and States collecting State GST (SGST). In every invoice both CGST and SGST had to be separately shown and the taxes so collected paid separately into the account of the Centre and States. The GST on inter-State trade (IGST) was to be separately collected. In this scheme of things, the SGST did not directly impact inter-State trade. Therefore the basic architecture of GST and its input credit chain is not affected by giving States the option to choose a particular SGST within a narrow band. Though VAT had introduced uniform tax rates throughout India, in practice, there existed minor variations between States. It was the general understanding that this flexibility would be carried into the GST.

Another key issue was the rate of apportionment of the GST rates between the Centre and States. Many States had adopted a consistent position during the discussions in the Empowered Committee that the apportionment of rates of GST between the Centre and the States should be 60:40. The basis of this argument was that the proportion of State taxes subsumed was 44 per cent as against 28 per cent in the case of the Centre. The Centre also still has other buoyant sources of tax revenue, while the States would lose because the standard rate of tax of the States would fall substantially and compensation is only for five years. This logic for the apportionment of GST rates in a 60:40 ratio between the States and the Centre had been recognized by the Government of India Committee on Revenue Neutral Rates. On distribution of the Revenue Neutral Rate between the Union and States, the Report of the Committee on Revenue Neutral Rates headed by the then Chief Economic Advisor noted that the allocation of the rate 'must reflect the revenue requirements of the Centre and States so that revenues are protected. For example, a standard rate of 17 per cent would lead to rates at the Centre and States of say 8 per cent and 9 per cent, respectively because that is roughly the ratio of GST revenues that would have to be generated by the Centre and States assuming that the 2013-14 data on which these estimates are calculated remain valid. According to the committee it would be preferable to keep all other rates identical between the Centre and States to minimize distortions and facilitate compliance' (2015b, pp. 30-31).

Yet, the final decision has gone against the States with the equal apportionment of GST rates (on a 50:50 basis) between the Centre and the States. Now most of the commodities which were taxed at 14.5 per cent in the States are taxed at 9 per cent, which is 50 per cent of the 18 per cent GST. This is however on a base which is devoid of CST and Union excise duty.

A third set of issues relating to GST and the rights of States was that concerning tax administration. What would be the relative role of the State and central tax departments in administration of the new tax? The threshold limit for central excise was Rs 1.5 crores and therefore the discussions in the Empowered Committee almost took it for granted that smaller suppliers with turnover less than Rs 1.5 crores would be within the primary domain of the State administrations while the States and Centre would share the larger suppliers equally. The data crucial to the implementation of the new tax would be managed by a public limited company whose shares were equally held by the States and the Centre.

There was near consensus in the Empowered Committee on the above issues until the middle of 2010. Then initially a few BJP State governments led by Madhya Pradesh began to dissent protesting that the GST infringed on the States' interests.[2] Despite the fact

[2] The decision of Madhya Pradesh opposing GST has been reported in *Business Standard*, January 21, 2013, as 'The state cabinet is of the opinion that the central government wants to enter into the State tax domain and (into) powers to levy taxes granted by the Constitution. Moreover the central government has an intention to strip the state of autonomy in levying tax.' The cabinet decided to oppose the Centre's GST Bill as drafted, particularly the provisions that empower the central government to levy taxes which

that the BJP had included GST in its election manifesto, very soon all the BJP States including Gujarat joined hands to block further actions on GST implementation. However, the BJP reversed its position after it came to power at the Centre in 2014. Paradoxically, agreement on all the issues that had been raised in the Empowered Committee and around which a broad consensus had emerged was given short shrift and the final architecture of the GST turned out to be a serious blow to the fiscal rights of the States.

Once the constitutional amendments had become a reality, there was little room left for manoeuvrability and bargaining power. Alternative views were marginalized in the GST Council as the political landscape in the States changed in favour of the ruling party at the Centre. Besides, the constitutional structure of the GST Council as per the provisions of Article 279A itself makes States unequal partners with the Centre. The Centre has one third and all States have two thirds voting rights, but for a resolution to be passed in the GST Council, three fourths majority is required. In other words, the Centre has effective veto power in the GST Council. This is a new asymmetric feature added to our constitutional framework on Centre–State relations through the 101st amendment.

REVENUE NEUTRALITY OF GST RATES

The impact of GST in worsening the vertical fiscal imbalances between the Centre and the States is now a substantial negative factor outweighing the initial positive expectations of even those who were not in favour of doing what was done by the Empowered Committee of State Finance Ministers through a constitutional provision.

The first issue that was to be resolved before the implementation of GST was to fix Revenue Neutral Rates (RNR) for taxing goods and services subsumed under the GST, so that there is no fall in

come under State domain.

revenues due to the new rates vis-à-vis the old rates in the subsumed taxes. This necessitated a lot of discussions. Under the VAT regime, States were taxing almost 75 per cent of goods at the 14.5 per cent rate. A shift to GST would also remove the cascading effects in the tax base under the VAT regime (which included Central Excise, Service tax and CST). In effect, GST is levy of a lower rate on a smaller base. This has to be considered while deciding upon the revenue neutral rate.

The present rates in the GST are 0, 0.25, 3, 5, 12, 18 and 28 per cent respectively. With the GST Council decision to move a substantial number of taxable goods and services to 18 per cent rates from 28 per cent, the standard rate under which most goods and services are taxed is now 9 per cent each for the Centre and the States. Presently, the rate under which more than 80 per cent of goods and services are taxed are 18 and 12 per cent respectively. The standard rate under the GST regime is 18 per cent. This implies that the standard rate for the States has now fallen to 9 per cent. This is in principle and in practice not revenue neutral for the States. The Centre still has many other buoyant direct taxes and customs duty, whereas States do not have any substantial revenue elastic taxes that are not subsumed in GST. The tax on petroleum products can be subsumed in GST, if the GST Council decides to do so. So the reduction of the standard rate would permanently affect own tax revenues of the States adversely.

The clamour for merging the present multi-rate GST into a single rated one if needed to, would result in further deterioration of GST revenue collections. As we have seen, even with the present structure, there is a substantial rate fall for most of the commodities. If there is movement to a single rate, GST would lose even the semblance of progressivity in an otherwise regressive indirect tax. Tax rates on consumer durables and urban consumer products are the ones which have seen the sharpest decline. It is these same products which would further gain if the demand for a maximum ceiling rate of 18 per cent is accepted. The problem of multiplicity of rates is exaggerated. One only needs to think of the rate structure that existed before GST to realize the extent to which the tax structure has been simplified. Given the mass poverty and high level of income inequality in the country, it is preposterous to suggest a common rate of tax for grain flour and luxury vehicles. The ideal of equity should be considered at least as important as the ease of doing business.

An important issue that needs mention is the new burden of compliance on small traders.[3] The basic exemption limit under the previous central excise was upto Rs 1.5 crore. With GST, the Centre will be able to tax upto retail sales above the exemption limit of Rs 20 lakh. Dealers having turnover up to Rs 1.5 crore can now opt for composition scheme (earlier the limit was Rs 75 lakh), but they cannot get input tax credit for purchases from registered dealers. This would restrict their purchase choices and could compel the small traders who fall within limits of composition levy also to opt for the regular procedure and the rigours associated with it. Though this is a hardship for the smaller dealers, it is a substantial expansion of the tax base for Union.

As noted earlier, the equal apportionment of GST rates between the Centre and the States is not revenue neutral for the latter. As far as the States are concerned, there is an expansion in their tax base by the inclusion of service tax, which is currently levied by the Centre. The proportion of State taxes subsumed under GST is 44 per cent (Sales Tax/VAT is 78 per cent of Own Tax Revenue and VAT is 53 per cent of Sales Tax + VAT).[4] It is also to be noted that States do not have any buoyant source left after the commodities

[3] However, there has been an amendment which has negated the requirement for reverse charges in the case of unregistered dealers.

[4] This is based on Kerala's finances and the situation in other States is more or less similar.

subject to VAT are subsumed under GST. In this context, the rate of apportionment of rates between CGST and SGST and the States' necessity for a higher share than that of the Centre assumes significance. The following illustration will explain the present and post-GST scenario.

The following illustrative examples would reveal how the equal apportionment of GST rates is not revenue-neutral for the States.

NON REVENUE-NEUTRAL GST RATES: ILLUSTRATIONS

Let us assume that a good with a retail price of Rs 100 (before Central Excise and VAT) is subject to excise duty of 12.5 per cent at the ex-factory price of Rs 75 and 14.5 per cent State VAT at the retail price Rs 100. Let us also assume that the taxable service element in this commodity is Rs 10, at 15 per cent rate, it works out to Rs 2.25 and this accrues entirely to the Centre. The combined effective rate in this case is calculated as follows:

a) The excise duty at 12.5 per cent of Rs 75 is Rs 9.375 and that is 9.375 per cent of the final Rs 100. Inclusive of service tax of Rs 2.25 the total works out to Rs 11.625.

b) The VAT at 14.5 per cent of Rs 100 (without considering the cascading effect of VAT on excise duty) is Rs 14.5.

c) The combined rate of Excise Duty, Service Tax and VAT on Rs 100 is 26.125 per cent (11.625 per cent plus 14.5 per cent).

Under GST the combined rate recommended by the GST Council is 5, 12, 18 and 28 per cent (plus cess) respectively. It is expected that a majority of goods will fall under the 12 and 18 per cent respectively. The above illustration justifies bifurcation of CGST and SGST in the ratio of Union 11.625 per cent and State 14.5 per cent.

a) In case of 12 per cent GST

Union Share (CGST) will be 12 x 11.625/26.125 = 5.33 per cent, rounded to 5 per cent.

States' share (SGST) will be 12 x 14.5/26.125 = 6.66 per cent, rounded to 7 per cent.

b) In case of 18 per cent GST

Union Share (CGST) will be 18 x 11.625/26.125 = 8.009 per cent, rounded to 8 per cent.

States' share (SGST) will be 18 x 14.5/26.125 = 9.99 per cent, may be rounded to 10 per cent.

It is worth mentioning here that though under a different rate structure (of uniform 12 per cent and more commodities being subsumed), the Task Force constituted by the 13th Finance Commission suggested that the SGST rate should be higher by 2 per cent than CGST rate (Ramalingam 2017).

IMPLEMENTATION OF GST: ISSUES AFFECTING STATES AND STAKEHOLDERS

To add to these shortcomings, the implementation of GST has been affected by a plethora of problems. Some of the major issues deserving mention are:

a) Despite the sharp reduction in the incidence of tax burden under the GST regime there was no reduction in the Maximum Retail Prices (MRP) but for a few commodities. The reduction of tax only resulted in windfall gains for corporates and traders at the expense of the consumers. The anti-profiteering clause (Section 171 of the CGST Act, 2017) was not implemented along with GST and this left the consumer who was exploited by certain traders without any statutory forum to voice grievances. The State governments

Table 5.1: GST collection during August 2017-May 2018 (Rs crore)

Month	GST Collection
August 2017	93,590
September 2017	92,029
October 2017	95,132
November2017	85,931
December 2017	83,716
January 2018	88,929
February 2018	88,047
March2018	89,264
April 2018	1,03,457
May 2018	94,016

Source: *Press Information Bureau*, Government of India.

forwarded complaints to the Centre but no effective action could be taken. The general perception has been one of increase in the tax because the GST rates printed on the invoices were invariably higher than the erstwhile VAT rates.

b) The IGST Act, 2017, (section 18) provided that States would get their SGST share only when a dealer having inter-State trade pays output tax, files return and claims credit for input tax. In other words, IGST (which is CGST + SGST) which is paid in inter-State trade remains with the Centre which acts as a clearing house for States which are destinations of supply of goods and services and only subsequently trickles down to the States. This results in the States' share in IGST remaining with the Centre for a considerable time, creating liquidity problems for the States and forcing them to borrow money and pay interest while their dues are available as interest free ways and means for the Centre. IGST Act, 2017, needs an amendment to provide for provisional apportionment of the States' share without elapse of time.

c) The major disappointment was the functioning of the GSTN and the lacklustre performance of the IT backbone. For a whole year, tax collection was based on a summary statement submitted by taxpayers (GSTR 3B) from which it is not possible to verify the veracity of the

Figure 5.1: Trends in GST collection August 2017- May 2018 (Rs crore)

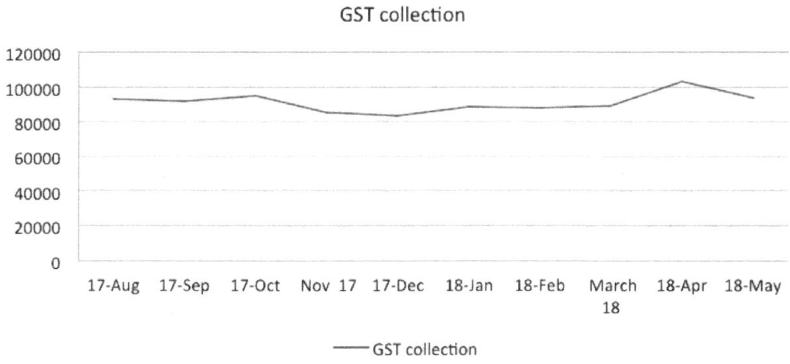

Source: Table 5.1

input credit claims, which is generally believed to be excessive. The GST Council is yet to decide upon the final format of tax returns. Not only has this led to substantial leakage of revenue but also piling up of the export refunds.

d) The delay in implementation of E-Way bill[5]and immediate abolition of checkposts have resulted in substantial tax evasion, especially in inter-State trade, where there was no effective mechanism to check flow of goods in the interregnum between the abolition of checkposts and implementation of the E-Way bill system. This is evident from the volatile trends in GST revenue during the first year of its implementation (Table 5.1).

e) The return forms prescribed for compliance have been seen as complicated by the taxpayers. From the enforcement angle, the IT network was not in place and this resulted in incomplete linking of output tax paid and input tax credit claimed by the taxpayers. The ad hoc system put in place wherein input tax credit was self-claimed, could not satisfy the test of self-compliance, as it adversely affected invoice level credit matching. The complications in return filing have now been recognized by the GST Council and a committee of

[5] E-way bill is necessary for all transactions above Rs 50,000.

ministers has been formed for simplifying the return filing procedure. The system is yet to be put in place completely.

The impediments in implementation and frequent rate changes have resulted in volatile trends in GST collection (Table 5.1 and Figure 5.1) and revenue generation below expectations.

The GST rates did not stabilize in the initial year of implementation and there were frequent changes in them, which created expectations of further changes in future and impeded the implementation of a sustainable tax system. As already stated, return filing under GST has proved to be cumbersome for small traders and there have been moves to simplify the same. Many important provisions were not implemented along with GST and are only now being put in place. These have led to a situation where afterthought was taking precedence over careful planning before implementation.

These statutory and implementation issues have reduced the effectiveness of GST, which has also eroded the constitutional rights of the States. If the present costs of erosion of States' taxing powers originally envisaged under the Constitution, more than outweigh the expected revenue gains and enhanced spending capabilities, the tenets of this tax reform would become unacceptable in the medium run. This would in turn lead to a call for revising the framework and implementation procedure of GST.

Though many viewed GST critically as it took away the constitutional power of the States to vary tax rates even within a narrow band, they were willing or rather compelled to accept GST, as it was expected to bring in more revenues due to expansion of the tax base and through self-compliance. These were in turn expected to enable the States, which were facing a slowdown in VAT revenue growth, to allocate more resources for social sector and capital expenditures. In practice, the expected benefit from a larger tax base outweighed the loss consequent to the erosion of the inherent principle of fiscal federalism, which enabled sub-national entities to fix their tax rates. The incursion into States' fiscal domain that the statutory features and implementation of the GST have involved has dampened the expectations of even reasoned critics.

In the prevailing context, vertical fiscal imbalances between the Centre and the States are worsening and it goes counter to building a healthy democratic and federal polity. This would in turn shrink social sector spending leading to adverse impact on human development indicators, inclusive economic growth,[6] and fiscal disempowerment of the states. There is need for a substantial shift in the attitude of the Centre with regard to ameliorating vertical imbalances in the larger interests of the federal and democratic fabric of the country. It is in this context that we analyse the ToR of the 15th FC and their likely impact on the already widening vertical fiscal imbalances between the Centre and the States.

[6] See Mitra (1987) for a discussion of the adverse impact of centralization on economic growth.

CHAPTER 6

TERMS OF REFERENCE OF 15TH FINANCE COMMISSION: IMPLICATIONS

As argued above, the FCs which are constitutional bodies with the primary mandate of ameliorating vertical fiscal imbalances, along with equalizing fiscal capacities of States to the extent possible, are being burdened with additional ToRs, which essentially are a means to implement fiscal targeting in tune with the neoliberal agenda. The clauses in the ToR of the 15th FC have spurred a controversy with opposition from some State governments and critical discussion in the public domain for its anti-federal and undemocratic tenor, prompting a group of State finance ministers to meet and submit a memorandum to the President of India requesting deletion of certain items of the ToR. It is in the context of this unprecedented development that we examine the implications of the ToR of the 15th FC, by placing them in the economic and political background of the prevailing division of powers in the Indian federation.

MANDATE OF THE 15TH FC: A COMPARATIVE OVERVIEW

The 15th FC has been appointed at a time when the Indian federal architecture is undergoing unprecedented change. Among the shifts are the abolition of the Planning Commission, introduction of GST, review of the FRBM by a committee mandated to suggest changes and the award of the 14th FC. In this context, before we enter into the issues related to the ToR of the 15th FC, it will be appropriate to examine the constitutional mandate of any FC. As already stated the Constitution prescribes the appointment of FCs, every quinquennium by the President, as per provisions of Article 280, which are extracted below:

> 280. (1) The President shall, within two years from the commencement of this Constitution and thereafter at the expiration of every fifth year or at such earlier time as the President considers necessary, by order constitute a Finance Commission which shall consist of a Chairman and four other members to be appointed by the President.
>
> (2) Parliament may by law determine the qualifications which shall be requisite for appointment as members of the Commission and the manner in which they shall be selected.
>
> (3) It shall be the duty of the Commission to make recommendations to the President as to –
>
> (a) the distribution between the Union and the States of the net proceeds of taxes which are to be, or may be, divided between them under this Chapter and the allocation between the States of the respective shares of such proceeds;
>
> (b) the principles which should govern the grants-in-aid of the revenues of the States out of the Consolidated Fund of India;
>
> [(bb) the measures needed to augment the Consolidated Fund of a State to supplement the resources of the Panchayats in the State on the basis of the recommendations made by the Finance Commission of the State;]
>
> [(c) the measures needed to augment the Consolidated Fund of a State to supplement the resources of the Municipalities in the State on the basis of the recommendations made by the Finance Commission of the State;]
>
> [(d)] any other matter referred to the Commission by the

President in the interests of sound finance.

(4) The Commission shall determine their procedure and shall have such powers in the performance of their functions as Parliament may by law confer on them.

It is clear from the above that the main intent of the Article is to make recommendations on sharing of net proceeds of taxes and principles governing grants-in-aid. There is also a provision under which the President can refer any other matter in the interests of sound finance. The definition or scope of the term sound finance is not elaborated in the Constitution. But the ToRs of the FCs since the 1990s have been continuously expanded by stretching this provision and imposing restrictions and conditionalities on the States. This trend has reached new heights in the ToR of the 15th FC, which is to make recommendations for the period 2020-21 to 2024-25. Incentivizing deficit targeting has been evident in the recommendations of all FCs since the 11th. Recently, there have been attempts to restrict expenditure priorities of the State governments, which is a clear incursion into the democratic domain of elected governments.

The ToR of the 14th FC had included an item 6(viii) that mandated

> the need for insulating the pricing of public utility services like drinking water, irrigation, power and public transport from policy fluctuations through statutory provisions.

This was a clear attempt to enter into the political decision-making arena of democratically-elected governments. But the ToR of the 14th FC did not explicitly mention this as regarding the States. It apparently applied to the Union government also. The 14th FC, however, did not make any specific recommendation on this ToR.

Table 6.1: A comparative view of ToR of 14th and 15th FCs

Item number in ToR	14th Finance Commission	15th Finance Commission	Remarks
5 (14th & 15th)	The Commission shall review the state of the finances, deficit and debt levels of the Union and the States, keeping in view, in particular, the fiscal consolidation road map recommended by the Thirteenth Finance Commission, and suggest measures for maintaining a stable and sustainable fiscal environment consistent with equitable growth including suggestions to amend the Fiscal Responsibility and Budget Management Acts currently in force and while doing so, the Commission may consider the effect of the receipts and expenditure in the form of grants for creation of capital assets on the deficits; and the Commission shall also consider and recommend incentives and disincentives for States for observing the obligations laid down in the Fiscal Responsibility and Budget Management Acts.	The Commission shall review current status of finance, deficit, debt levels cash balance and fiscal discipline efforts of the Union and the States, and recommend a fiscal consolidation road map for sound fiscal management, taking into account the responsibility of the Central Government and State Governments to adhere to appropriate levels of general and consolidated government debt and deficit levels, while fostering higher inclusive growth in the country, guided by the principles of equity, efficiency and transparency. The Commission may also examine whether revenue deficit grants be provided at all.	The words 'stable and sustainable fiscal environment consistent with equitable growth' are absent in the ToR of the 15th FC. The mandate to make recommendations on whether 'Revenue Deficit grants should be provided at all' is making its appearance in the ToR of 15th FC for the first time.

6(vi) of 14th and 7(iv) and (v) of 15th	The level of subsidies that are required, having regard to the need for sustainable and inclusive growth, and equitable sharing of subsidies between the Central Government and State Governments;	(iv) Progress made in increasing capital expenditure, eliminating losses of power sector, and improving the quality of such expenditure in generating future income streams; (v) Progress made in increasing tax/non-tax revenues, promoting savings by adoption of Direct Benefit Transfers and Public Finance Management System, promoting digital economy and removing layers between the government and the beneficiaries;	The ToR of the 15th FC proposes to look at only the States' case for performance grants, whereas the Union is left out unlike in the ToR of 14th FC.
6(vii) of 14th FC and 7(vii) of 15th FC	The need for insulating the pricing of public utility services like drinking water, irrigation, power and public transport from policy fluctuations through statutory provisions;	Control or lack of it in incurring expenditure on populist measures;	Though both try to insulate certain budgetary decisions from the political domain, the scope of the ToR of 14th FC is far more limited than that of the 15th FC ToR which is directly incursive into the domain of State governments and their legislative realm. The ToR of the 14th FC is not limited to the States only.

Note: Table continued overleaf.

7 of 14th FC and 8 of 15th FC	In making its recommendations on various matters, the Commission shall generally take the base of population figures as of 1971 in all cases where population is a factor for determination of devolution of taxes and duties and grants-in-aid; however, the Commission may also take into account the demographic changes that have taken place subsequent to 1971.	The Commission shall use the population data of 2011 while making its recommendations.	The ToR of the 15th FC is far more restrictive than that of the 14th FC and the word 'generally' is conspicuous by its absence in the ToR of 15th FC.
6(vi) of 15th FC	No comparable ToR	The impact on the fiscal situation of the Union Government of substantially enhanced tax devolution to States following recommendations of the 14th Finance Commission, coupled with the continuing imperative of the national development programme including New India-2022;	The review of the recommendations of an earlier Finance Commission, accepted and implemented, is a new and unprecedented feature in the ToR of the 15th FC. This can be an attempt to suggest reduction in percentage of taxes shareable with the States.

Source: 14th Finance Commission Report and Notification of Constitution of 15th Finance Commission.

The ToR of the 15th FC has been more explicit in having items which are tantamount to weakening the federal architecture. Item wise discussion of the ToR of the 15th FC would reveal the bias against the States when defining the mandate of the FC. This deviates from the spirit of the federal principles enshrined in the Constitution. An illustrative comparison between the ToR of the 14th and the 15th FCs clearly reveals the increasing tendency to weaken the federal structure and restrict the role of the FC as a constitutionally authorized arbitrator to ameliorate vertical and horizontal imbalances.

Amidst otherwise worsening vertical fiscal imbalances, one positive feature worth mentioning is the recommendation of the 10th FC that all Union taxes should be made shareable with the States. This was implemented by the 80th Constitution amendment and FCs from the 11th started devolving a share of all Union taxes. Prior to the 80th amendment, only personal income tax (less net proceeds attributable to Union territories and taxes on Union emoluments) was shareable under Article 270 of the Constitution. Central Excise duties were shareable by approval of Parliament under Article 272 of the Constitution. The change brought about by the 80th amendment accepted a long-standing demand of the States for a share of all Union taxes.

Gulati and George (1988) have made a detailed analysis of recommendations of the 6th, 7th and 8th FCs. They have highlighted the declining role of resource transfers by the FCs and the rise in share of other discretionary grants. The loans by Centre to the States, institutional finance and central inroads into State subjects have also been discussed. Since the 11th FC, there has been a paradigm shift in the recommendations as all taxes have become part of the divisible pool. Loans from the Centre have been declining and institutional finance has undergone a complete change as a result of market driven reforms and the shift to universal banking. But vertical imbalances are not only persisting but exacerbating.

ToR OF 15TH FC: ROLLING BACK THE LITTLE GAINS FROM THE 14TH FC AWARD

In spite of the worsening vertical fiscal imbalances between the Centre and the States, it needs to be mentioned that the 14th FC award attempted a change in Centre–State fiscal relations by providing a greater share of flexible resources to the States through increasing tax devolution and doing away with the practice of recommending specific grants. The share of the States in the divisible pool of taxes was raised from the 32 per cent awarded by the 13th FC to 42 per cent in the 14th FC award. But the paradigm shift in inter-governmental transfers was the abrogation of specific and performance-based grants in the recommendations of the 14th FC. It now appears that the approach of the 14th FC has not gone down well with the Union government as it has sought to neutralize a part of this increase by restructuring the grants. It is this that the ToR of the 15th FC attempts to roll back, so as to reverse the trend set in motion by the 14th FC award.

Alarmingly, ToR 6(iv) states that:

> While making its recommendations, the Commission shall have regard, among other considerations, to:
>
> The impact of the fiscal situation of the Union Government of substantially enhanced tax devolution to the States following recommendation of the 14th Finance Commission, coupled with the coming imperative of national development programme including New India-2022.

This is unprecedented and clearly transgresses the constitutional mandate of the FC. As pointed out earlier, the very statement that there was a 'substantial enhancement' from 32 per cent to 42 per cent in devolution of net proceeds of taxes collected by the Union to the States does not conform to reality. Though the increase in devolution is a fact, it needs to be taken note of that the 14th FC considered the entire revenue account and not only the non-plan revenue account. Besides, post-14th FC, the States are not getting Gadgil formula grants or NCA for their plans since 2015-16 and the central share in many of the CSS, classified as 'core schemes' has come down from 75 to 60 per cent, thereby increasing the States' share from 25 to 40 per cent. An ever increasing share of surcharges and cesses (Table 3.2) has diminished the divisible pool itself. These acts of the central government have made what is portrayed as 'substantial enhancement' in ToR 6(iv) into a merely incremental one.

Yet another idea repugnant to federalism in this ToR is the fact that it requires the 15th FC to take account of the central government's commitment to New India-2022, though most of the areas in that programme are in the State List. While implementing national priorities in a federal set up, the expenditure commitments of Centre, States and local governments are to be considered holistically as they are equal stakeholders. This issue has been raised by the group of finance ministers in their memorandum to the President and revision of the ToR is necessary.

ATTEMPT TO DO AWAY WITH POST-DEVOLUTION REVENUE DEFICIT (RD) GRANTS

Clause 5 of the ToR of the 15th Finance Commission mandates as under:

> The Commission shall review the current status of the finance, deficit, debt levels, cash balances and fiscal discipline efforts of the Union and the States, and recommend a fiscal consolidation roadmap for sound fiscal management, taking into account the responsibility

of the Central Government and State Governments to adhere to appropriate levels of general and consolidated government debt and deficit levels, while fostering higher inclusive growth in the country, guided by the principles of equity, efficiency and transparency. The Commission may also examine whether revenue deficit grants be provided at all.

The last sentence in the above quote from the ToR, mandates the 15th FC to recommend whether there should be RD grants at all. Till the 14th FC, post-tax devolution deficit grants under Article 275, were called Non-Plan Revenue Deficit (NPRD) grants. This was a very important source of flexible funds as part of central resource transfer and an important means for augmenting the Consolidated Fund of the States. As already mentioned, the 14th FC awarded RD grants taking a holistic view of plan and non-plan revenue expenditures. When the State finances are likely to be stressed in the immediate future due to a) pay commission awards, b) problems in implementation of GST c) spending requirements in social and economic sectors, and d) interest liabilities on UDAY bonds, the above ToR is a retrograde step and would severely strain State finances. There is also a constitutional issue that arises here. Article 280(3)(b) States that *it shall be duty of the FC to make recommendations on the principles governing grants-in-aid of the States out of the Consolidated Fund of India*. The grants-in-aid recommended on this basis are charged expenditure to the Consolidated Fund of India as per Article 275 of the Constitution. In view of the specific mandate in Article 280(3)(b) of the Constitution, the ToR 5 has clearly overstepped the constitutional mandate.

CONDITIONALITIES IMPOSED FOR BORROWING BY THE STATES

The ToR 5(vi) mandates determining conditions that the Government of India (GoI) may impose on States while providing consent under Article 293(3) of the Constitution (for market borrowings).

Already FRBM Acts have been passed by the State legislatures and limits for borrowings have been specified therein. The pertinent question is why further conditions are necessary? It is obviously a move to further restrain the borrowings and constrain the fiscal space of States. The Chairman of the 15th FC, while heading the FRBM Review Committee, had recommended a debt–GSDP limit of 60 per cent (40 for the Centre and 20 for the States). For this to be achieved, the FRBM committee recommended that the Centre's FD to GDP ratio should be 2.5 per cent by 2022-23 and all States at 1.7 per cent by 2022-23. The adverse fall out of this for State finances and the economy as a whole along with the unsound basis of these recommendations have been discussed elaborately in Chapter 4. This ToR is a pointer towards the attempt to impose these conditionalities by invoking provisions of Article 293(3) of the Constitution. This is uncalled for as there are already legislative restraints on borrowing. If further restrictive conditionalities are put, the fiscal space for capital expenditure of the States would be severely constrained with adverse consequences on economic growth.

MONITORING OF PERFORMANCE OF STATES THROUGH INCENTIVES

Clause 7 of the ToR of the 15th FC clearly turns the clock back on the 14th FC recommendations which did away with conditional and performance-based grants. The clause, in violation of constitutional principles, makes the FC a monitoring agency for implementation of central government policies. Bodies like the Inter-State Council (Article 263) can discuss how outcome budgets can be put in place by the State governments. The FC is not an ongoing body and any monitoring role attributed to it would soon turn into supervision of State governments by central officials. Clauses 7(i) to (ix) in the ToR, provide for measurable performance-based indicators, like widening of GST net, population control, power transmission losses, utilization of funds of CSS, promoting digital economy, ease of doing business, labour intensive growth, controlling populist measures etc. Clause 7(ix) further mandates measuring attributes such as behavioural change, which are beyond easy quantification.

Drawing/utilization of funds from flagship schemes by the States is also made a basis for providing performance-based incentives. When States are at different levels of development, the drawing/utilization of funds will not be the same for them, especially when the criteria in the flagship schemes are uniform across States, ignoring regional specificities. Making this a criterion for performance-based incentive is a double whammy for States which are not able to avail of the schemes due to lack of flexible criteria. This ToR clause is contrary to the federal principle of treating Centre, States and local governments as equal stakeholders.

While States are sought to be incentivized or penalized for drawal/non-drawal of funds from central flagship schemes (ToR 7(iii)), their own welfare schemes are sought to be controlled by terming them as 'populist'. This defies economic rationale as States being closer to the beneficiaries can design and implement welfare schemes better (as evident from the success of State-level schemes earlier). This discriminatory approach stems from a total lack of appreciation of the historical background from which the central flagship schemes emerged.

Most of the central flagship schemes had State-level predecessors. In fact, States had acted as testing laboratories for these schemes before they could be launched at the national level. The Mahatma Gandhi National Rural Employment Guarantee Act (MGNREGA) had a State-level food-for-work scheme as its precursor in Maharashtra. The noon meal scheme was implemented in States like Kerala and Tamil Nadu five decades before. Even decentralization to local bodies through the 73rd and 74th Constitution amendments were preceded by major State-level initiatives in Kerala, West Bengal and Karnataka. Had all these been dubbed as populist and sought to be controlled through the ToR of earlier FCs, it is doubtful whether we could have launched any central flagship schemes. These attempts to stifle the policy domain and expenditure priorities of the State governments are not only against the grain of fiscal federalism but also undemocratic. This is also against the spirit of the obligations of a welfare state, enshrined in the Directive Principles of the Constitution. The one-size-fits-all central flagship schemes are given precedence over schemes that can be formulated with flexibly devolved funds, whereas economic rationale demands otherwise. It is distressing that a democratically elected State government and its schemes are treated as inferior to that of the Union. This exposes the fact that talk of cooperative federalism is mere rhetoric.

In fact, conditional or tied grants have traversed a chequered course in the recent past. The 11th FC recommended withholding of grants based on fiscal performance and there was strident criticism of that recommendation. The 12th FC went back on this and linked debt relief to fiscal target achievement. The 13th FC suggested monitoring of grants to local governments with presentation of utilization certificates and the 14th FC relaxed it finding this of little use. In fact, the 14th FC did away with the practice of tied grants itself, except as a part of performance grants to local governments.

The ToR of the 15th FC seems to suggest a return to tied grants and monitoring of outcomes, which in effect amounts to moving away from the ideal of cooperative federalism.

It needs to be reiterated that such micro-level monitoring assigned in clause 7 of the ToR stretches the scope of 'any other matter referred to the Commission by the President in the interests of sound finance', envisaged under Article 280(3)(c) the Constitution, beyond reasonable limits.

CONTROL OR LACK OF IT IN INCURRING EXPENDITURE ON POPULIST SCHEMES: ToR 7(VIII)

Clause 7(viii) of the ToR speaks of controlling adoption of 'populist' measures by the States. This clause is not only anti-federal but undemocratic and needs to be separately highlighted. Through this clause the 15th FC is being given the authority to restrain democratically elected governments from implementing promises made to people in their election manifestoes. Any measure related to welfare pensions, food subsidy and public distribution system can be selected for control. This strikes at the root of democratic politics and brings a neoliberal anti-people agenda explicitly into the ToR, providing the FC with wide latitude to stride into the domain of electorally mandated democratic practice and policy making by sovereign State assemblies. This is a substantial incursion into the rights of elected State governments.

Besides, the ToR clause commented on above, there is clause 8 of the ToR of the 15th FC which prescribes using population numbers from the 2011 census while making its recommendations. This has a very serious adverse implication for many States, which have made progress in achieving goals set in the National Population Policy, 1977. Clause 8 of the ToR of the 15th FC is discussed in Chapter 7, dealing with horizontal fiscal imbalances and conflicting interests across States in India.

EXPANDING ToR: THEIR IMPLICATIONS

The attempt to make a constitutional body like the FC a vehicle for implementing deficit targeting and expenditure cuts, through additional ToR, which started with the adoption of neoliberal reforms has thus gathered momentum in the ToR of the 15th FC. As already stated, this is done by stretching the constitutional provision under Article 280(3)(d), enabling then President to refer *any other matter in the interest of sound finance.*

Isaac (2018a) points out that the ToR of the 15th FC has challenged the federal values enshrined in the Constitution and the modicum of fiscal autonomy State governments enjoy. It was further stated that even though there can be different opinions among States on ToR clause 8, which mandates the 15th FC to use population based on the 2011 census instead of the 1971 census, all the States have common concerns regarding clauses in the ToR dealing with the vertical distribution of resources between the Union and the States. Political reasons should not affect the national duty to defend the rights of States on the one hand and fiscal federalism in the country on the other hand, even while agreeing to disagree on criteria for *inter se* distribution of taxes between the States. It is relevant here to mention that the FC should be allowed to do its constitutional duty and the Centre must not micro-manage it by adding clauses that limit tax devolution, make borrowing power conditional, and so on (Isaac 2018b).

The domain experts' view is that States need to debate a number of contentious issues in the ToR which affect the very structure of fiscal federalism, like clause 5 of the ToR which mandates the FC 'to examine whether revenue deficit grants be provided at all'; clause 6(iv) which calls for examining 'the impact of [the] fiscal situation of the Union government of substantially enhanced devolution by the Fourteenth Finance Commission, coupled with continuing imperative of the national development programme including

New India-2022'; clause 5(vi) looking at the conditions that may be imposed by the central government while providing consent to States when they borrow under Article 293(3); and clause 7 asking the Commission to propose measurable performance-based incentives to States in respect of a number of areas such as the implementation of flagship schemes, progress towards replacement rate of population growth, control or lack of it in incurring expenditure on populist measures; and finally, promotion of ease of doing business. The issue is not one restricted to use of population based on the 2011 census. It has been further stated that though directives and guidelines have been issued to the FCs in the past also, the ToR of the 15th FC raise questions about constitutional propriety and has implications for the federal fabric of the nation itself (Rao 2018).

Oommen (2018) while commenting on clause 6(iv) of the ToR of the15th FC, states that it is improper for the ToR to express value judgements on earlier Commissions which in this case turns out to be a covert directive to the 15th FC to be cautious. If literally taken by the Commission, it will have serious consequences for local governments whose share was increased 3.5 times compared to the 13th FC. He further adds that nation building is not an exclusive project of the Centre, particularly when programme-wise targets and financial allocations remain unspecified.

If present trends are carried further at the accelerated phase suggested in the ToR of the 15th FC, the result would be erosion of whatever little flexible fiscal space States have and as a consequence the further weakening of the already fragile federal architecture in India. All talk of cooperative federalism seems to have evaporated into thin air. It is time that the States effectively take a position on these issues in their memorandums to the 15th FC, not only for retaining their rightful position in the federal polity, but for the federal policy itself to survive.

The ToR of the 15th FC, if not changed has the potential to substantially alter the system of inter-governmental fiscal transfers. The consequence of this would be that the States would find it difficult to pursue independent fiscal initiatives in future, which would be contrary to their expected role in a robust federal system. It appears that the basic constitutional foundation of having an FC is diluted through by the ever expanding ToR of the successive FCs. This has scaled new heights in the ToR of the 15th FC. It is a fact that our transfer system has several deficiencies that requires correction. But, it cannot be through increasing reliance on tied and conditional grants. Instead, an alternative, which accommodates and protects the objectives of equity, efficiency and autonomy of the States should be strived for.

CHAPTER 7

HORIZONTAL FISCAL IMBALANCES AND CONFLICTING INTERESTS OF STATES

IMPORTANCE OF EQUITY IN FINANCE COMMISSION TRANSFERS

The main task of the FC is to address the issue of vertical and horizontal fiscal imbalances. We have already discussed the issue of vertical fiscal imbalances in Chapter 3. In this chapter, we focus on the horizontal fiscal imbalances. While determining the *inter se* share of States, the basic aim of FCs has so far been to bridge the differentials in revenue raising capacity and cost disability factors, without giving rise to perverse incentives. To achieve these goals, different FCs have followed the principles of equity and efficiency with overwhelming importance given to indicators of equity. The criteria used by the FCs can be categorized as a) factors reflecting needs such as population and income distance, b) cost disability indicators such as area and infrastructure, and c) fiscal efficiency indicators such as tax effort and fiscal discipline. One of the key indicators of equity is population and there is broad agreement that population should be used as a one of the indicators for *inter se* distribution of taxes.

When the level of per capita incomes are highly unequal, it is not an easy task to arrive at a consensus on the indicators to be

Table 7.1: Weights for population and income distance, 11th to 14th FCs

FCs and their period	Weight for 1971 population (%)	Weight for per capita income distance (%)	Total (%)
11th 2000-01 to 2004-05	10	62.5	72.5
12th 2005-06 to 2009-10	25	50	75
13th 2010-11 to 2014-15	25	47.5	72.5
14th 2015-16 to 2019-20	17.5 (+10% for demographic changes proxied by 2011 population)	50	77.5

Source: Reports of the Finance Commissions.

used and the weightage to be given to them in the formula for *inter se* distribution of taxes.[1] In the Indian context, the combined weight of two main equity criteria, i.e. population and distance of per capita income, has consistently been around 75 per cent. The weights given to population and per capita income distance by the FCs since the 11th are given in Table 7.1.

The comparison starts with the 11th FC because prior to that only personal income tax and Union excise duties were shareable with the States. After the 80th Constitution amendment, all Union taxes except surcharges and cesses are shareable with the States and this has been in effect since the 11th FC.

The smaller and larger weights given by the 11th FC to population based on the 1971 census and per capita income distance respectively, led to strident protests from middle-income States like Kerala, Tamil Nadu, Andhra Pradesh, Karnataka etc., which had taken substantial measures in family welfare and had achieved replacement rates of population. The subsequent three FCs reduced the weight for income distance when compared with that of the 11th FC. The 14th FC introduced a 10 percentage weight for demographic changes since 1971 proxied by the 2011 population.

[1] Bharadwaj (1982) traces the imbalances to distortions in investments to serve colonial interests.

The use of population based on the 1971 census in the equity criteria was because measures aimed at limiting population growth were to be implemented with the adoption of the National Population Policy in 1977, through a Parliamentary resolution. The stated intention was to offer some relief to States which had made a conscious effort to achieve better demographic indicators and replacement ratios in keeping with that policy.

The highly populous and low per capita income States like Uttar Pradesh, Bihar, Madhya Pradesh and Rajasthan had higher shares even when population based on the 1971 census was used and hence the equity principle was not violated. Moreover, the current population size implicitly entered the criteria as the denominator in computing per capita incomes, which had almost 50 per cent weightage among all devolution criteria. The grants to local governments as mandated by Article 280(3)(bb) and (c) of the Constitution also took account of population based on the latest census. Finally, the 14th FC introduced the population based on the 2011 census in its criteria, as its ToR had mandated it to consider demographic changes since 1971, but retained population based on the 1971 census with a higher weightage than that for the population based on the 2011 census.

However, clause 8 of the ToR of the 15th FC has mandated the use of population based on the 2011 census while making its recommendations. This has given rise to genuine apprehensions among many States which, because of demographic advance, have recorded a decline in the share of their population in total national population between 1971 and 2011. While there cannot be any disagreement with the view that highly populous and low per capita income States should get a higher share in tax devolution, that cannot result in a situation in which the share of States with demographic achievements fall precipitously. This would amount to them being penalized for implementing the National Population

Table 7.2: Loss in tax share to States had 14th FC used only 2011 Population (%)

State	Share as per 14th FC award	Share with 14th FC criteria and only 2011 population	Loss
Andhra Pradesh	4.308	4.280	-0.168
Goa	0.374	0.367	-0.007
Gujarat	3.085	3.023	-0.062
Karnataka	4.715	3.442	-1.273
Kerala	2.501	1.713	-0.788
Maharashtra	5.522	5.139	-0.388
Tamil Nadu	4.024	3.685	-0.339
Telangana	2.438	2.107	-0.331
Uttarakhand	1.052	0.967	-0.085
West Bengal	7.33	6.707	-0.623

Source: 14th Finance Commission Report, mospi.gov.in, own computations.

Policy, 1977, with all earnestness and incurring a fiscal burden for the same.

The loss to the States which are adversely affected by this criterion is quite substantial as can be seen from Table 7.2, which computes the hypothetical loss in share of these States if the 14th Finance Commission had used only population based on the 2011 census.[2]

The ten States considered would substantially lose out on tax shares if the 14th FC criteria are applied using only 2011 population estimates. It could be argued that some States would gain also. But equity is an encompassing and not a divisive concept. If some States lose substantially only because they have achievements in health and education to their credit, which changes their demographic indicators in ways that affect taxes shares adversely, nothing can be more contrary to logic and reason. As already pointed out, even when population based on the 1971 census is used, the more populous States do get a larger share of devolved taxes. And, if they need to be given more in the interest of fiscal equalization, grants under Article 275, which are for State specific needs, can be

[2] In this illustration, per capita income distance is calculated based on an average of GSDP at current prices for 2013-14, 2014-15 and 2015-16.

utilized for the purpose. In such a case, their resource shares can go up without prejudicing the tax share of the ten States, which stand to lose heavily if population based on the 2011 census is used. This simple reasoning seems to have been missed while framing the ToR of the 15th FC. On the other hand, ToR 5 goes beyond the constitutional mandate and requires the 15th FC to consider whether Article 275 grants should be made at all.

The point that needs to be underscored is that the FC as a constitutional body and a neutral arbitrator should have the space to decide how the equalization of fiscal capacity is to be best achieved. Earlier, population based on the 1971 census was mentioned in the ToR because of the National Population Policy which was passed by a Parliamentary resolution. This principle is followed for delimitation of Lok Sabha and Assembly constituencies also. When this is sought to be done away with without any discussion with the States, all talk of cooperative federalism loses its meaning. The wording of ToR 8 is very restrictive. It states that 'The Commission shall use the Population data of 2011 while making its recommendations'. It would be worthwhile to compare that with the corresponding item in the ToR of the 14th FC which states as under:

> In making its recommendations on various matters, the Commission shall generally take the base of population figures as of 1971 in all cases where population is a factor for determination of devolution of taxes and duties and grants-in-aid; however, the Commission may also take into account the demographic changes that have taken place subsequent to 1971.

It can be clearly seen that the ToR 8 of the 15th FC is highly restrictive when compared to the ToR of the 14th FC and constricts the room available for the FC to balance the interests of the States with differing fiscal capacities. There is a substantial difference between 'shall generally take, . . . may also take into account' and 'shall use'. The latter provides zero degrees of freedom to the FC and is anti-federal in nature.

Agreement among the Union and the States to the maximum extent possible is the founding spirit of cooperative federalism. The FC has a constitutional role to perform in this regard. The framing of such restrictive ToR by the Centre is tantamount to destroying the spirit of cooperative federalism and creates apprehensions in the minds of States. When a general formula is applied, some States can lose and others can gain. It is here that the constitutional safeguard of Article 275 which provides for taking into account needs of different States and provide different sums as grants assumes importance. Clause 5 of the ToR of the 15th FC seems to have ignored this by requiring the Commission to review whether revenue deficit grants should be there at all. The constitutional intention to achieve fiscal equalization has been completely overlooked.

It is in these unprecedented circumstances that six States have jointly appealed to the President of India for reconsideration of certain items of the ToR of the 15th FC which are repugnant to the intentions of the Constitution, against the principles of cooperative federalism and intruding into the policy domain of elected State governments. The part of the joint memorandum to the President, requesting deletion of ToR 8, is pertinent as it addresses a multitude of issues arising from this ToR and is cited below:

> This direction represents a significant change in the ToR made after forty years. Starting a from the Seventh Finance Commission (1980-85) till the Fourteenth Finance Commission (2015-2020), eight Finance Commissions have been mandated to use the 1971 population for the purpose of computing States' shares and have complied with such mandate. The 15th FC is the first FC which has in its ToR the injunction to use the 2011 population census.

Population is an important criterion which significantly affects a state's share of the devolution pool. This is because it enters the computation of state shares both directly and indirectly. The 14th Finance Commission allotted a weight of 17.5% to 1971 population. Directly, 17.5% of a state's share in the divisible pool was determined on the basis of its 1971 population. Indirectly, the population figure was also used to scale the Income Distance criterion (to which it had allotted a weight of 50%). The explicit and implicit use of population in Finance Commission computations has a marked effect on state shares of the devolution pool.

The direction to the 15th FC to use the 2011 population figures is not appropriate for the following four reasons:

i. Over the last four decades the 1971 population has been used as a criterion for determining the states' share of the divisible pool by successive Finance Commissions even though subsequent census figures were available to it. The direction to the 15th Finance Commission to use the 2011 census figures militates against the Revised Policy Statement on the Family Welfare Programme placed before Parliament in June 1977 that guaranteed that the 1971 population figures will be used as the parameter for computing State devolution shares. This assurance was confirmed by the National Development Council in its meeting in 1979 and reiterated in the National Population Policy in 2000. The drastic change in population base from 1971 to 2011 proposed in the ToR should have been made after consultation with the NDC or at least the NITI Aayog which has accepted the principle of cooperative federalism as one of its operational tenets. One of the basic tenets of cooperative federalism is the need for all federating members to provide credible commitments to each other. Without any formal consultation with the states, this change belies the commitment given by the Centre to the states in 1977, 1979 and 2000 and weakens its capacity to make credible commitments in future.

ii. Income distance has been used as a criterion for horizontal devolution over the last seven finance commissions. The 15th FC may find it difficult to discard or substantially modify this criterion. This criterion represents the Commission's attempt to ensure states have the fiscal capacity to provide comparable levels of public services to their residents at comparable levels of taxation. This parameter is somewhat correlated to the 2011 population and thus meets the criticism that the use of the 1971 population is not realistic, since the 14th FC used the average of the 2010-11, 2011-12 and 2012-13 populations in determining it. This parameter provides greater weightage to poorer states depending upon the distance of their per capita GSDP from that of a rich state (Haryana in the case of the 14th FC). Placing high importance on equity, the 14th FC provided a weightage of 50% to the income distance criterion. If the 2011 population had been used for computations, the five states of Uttar Pradesh, Bihar, Madhya Pradesh, West Bengal, and Rajasthan would have got an aggregate weightage of 32.48% out of the 50% weight accorded to income distance to all the 29 states. Thus nearly 65% of the income distance criterion would have been pre-empted by these five states. The use of the 2011 population thus imposes a double whammy on the 'non-poor' states, who will be disadvantaged twice over.

iii. Trust between the federating members is also an essential component of a vibrant federation. Trust endures when changes from the norm are discussed between federating members in advance and the approach to be adopted is agreed upon if not unanimously then at least by majority. This has not been done while preparing the ToR of the 15th Finance Commission. The Centre has already belied the trust of the State governments in the case of payment of CST compensation and now the unilateral adoption of the 2011 population figures may further dilute this trust.

iv. Predictability is an important element of resource flows across inter-governmental units. State governments have not been subjected to severe fluctuations in their share of devolution in the past. Adoption of the 2011 Census figures by the 15th FC in its devolution formula may bring in unnecessary and undesirable volatility in horizontal devolution to states.

It has been argued that the 15th FC in its recommendations can dilute the effect of this provision by lowering the weightage it gives to the population parameter in the horizontal devolution formula. This argument is fallacious since as pointed out earlier, population enters the horizontal devolution formula in two ways – directly as a parameter and indirectly as a scaling factor. While the direct impact of population can be reduced by lowering its weightage, the indirect impact of population as a scaling factor will remain and this will continue to have a significant impact on the shares of our states.

This needs to be considered with the seriousness it deserves to preserve the very sanctity of the FC and its recommendations. The adverse impact of ToR 8 on federal relations transcends any one realm and this item in the ToR needs to be deleted to allay the genuine fears succinctly expressed by the States in their joint memorandum to the President.

CENTRAL TAXES AND GRANTS: DIFFERENTIAL IMPACTS ON PROGRESSIVITY

In this context, it would be worthwhile to analyse the impact of tax devolution and central grants with regard to their progressivity, which requires that there must be an inverse correlation between fiscal capacity and the amount of resource transfers. Gulati and George (1988), have discussed in detail the awards of the 6th, 7th and 8th FCs and their differential impact on States and drawn the conclusion that progressivity in the criteria was getting diluted.

When States are grouped on the basis of per capita Gross State Domestic Product (GSDP), it is seen that during the period 1980-

Table 7.3: Tax share among 15 major states, 1980-2015

Period	High	Middle	Low	
1980-85	17.59	33.23	49.18	100
1985-90	14.18	33.38	52.44	100
1990-95	14.6	33.12	52.28	100
1995-2000	14.12	33.79	52.09	100
2000-05	11.5	32.92	55.57	100
2005-2009	13.24	31.50	55.26	100
2010-2015	17.06	26.15	56.78	100

Source: *State Finances: A Study of Budgets*, RBI and *RBI Bulletin*, various issues.

Table 7.4: Grant share among 15 major States, 1980-2015

Period	High	Middle	Low	
1980-85	17.44	29.48	53.07	100
1985-90	19.43	31.64	46.73	98
1990-95	15.46	30.44	54.11	100
1995-2000	17.88	34.43	47.68	100
2000-05	19.82	39.04	41.15	100
2005-2009	23.54	34.74	41.71	100
2010-2015	24.36	30.58	45.06	100

Source: *State Finances: A Study of Budgets*, RBI and *RBI Bulletin*, various issues.

81 to 2005-06 the devolution of taxes has had an equalizing impact. The share of lower-income States had gone up and that of high-income States had fallen (Table 7.3). This could be due to the change in criteria of devolution adopted by the FCs by excluding collection from a State from the formula for tax devolution. Another feature to be noted is the stagnant share of the middle-income States throughout and a minor fall in their share during 2000-05 (Table 7.3), the period of the 11th FC (Mohan and Shyjan 2009). It is also observed that during 1980-81 to 2005-06, there was a perceptible fall in the share of the low-income states in total grants, whereas that of the middle-income States had risen considerably. There is also a minor increase in the case of high-income States (Table 7.4).

When the last one decade is separately analysed, it is seen that during the period 2005-06 to 2009-10 and during 2011-12 to 2014-15, taxes have had a more equalizing effect than grants. The

Figure 7.1: Share in Central taxes among 15 major States, 1980-2015

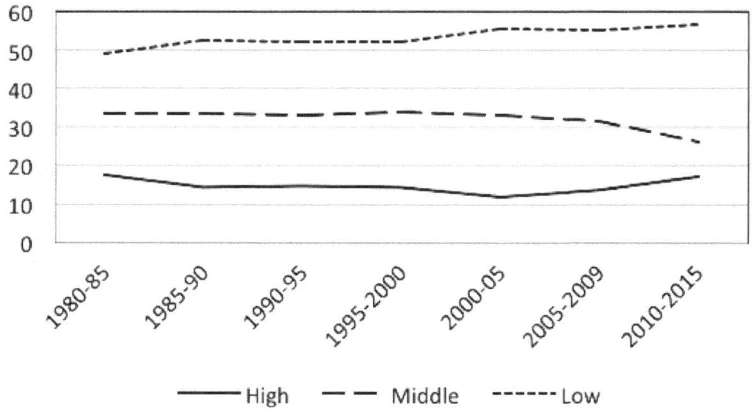

Source: Table 7.3.

Figure 7.2: Share in Central grants among 15 major States, 1980-2015

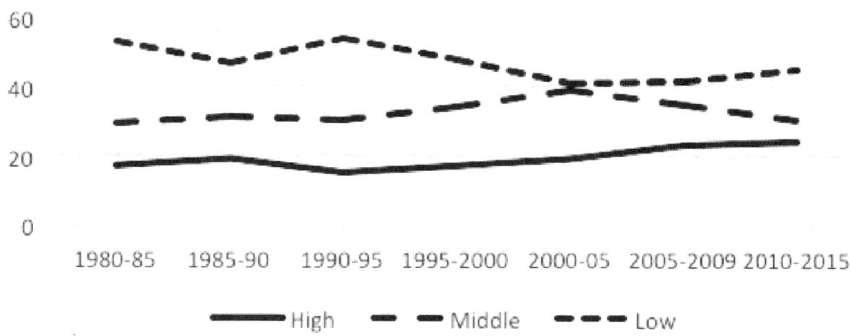

Source: Table 7.4.

correlation of taxes with per capita income for 15 major States is -0.81 and -0.79 respectively during the two time periods, indicating a mild decline in progressivity during the second five year period. The correlation coefficient of central grants with per capita income has been constant at -0.55 during 2005-06 to 2009-10 as well as 2010-11 to 2014-15, which is much less than that of taxes (Tables 7.5, 7.6, 7.7 and 7.8).

When 15 major States are grouped into high-, low- and middle-

Table 7.5: Share of Central taxes among 15 major States, 2005-06 to 2009-10

State	Rank in tax share	Rank in per capita income
Andhra Pradesh	3	9
Bihar	2	15
Goa	15	1
Gujarat	11	4
Haryana	14	2
Karnataka	10	8
Kerala	12	7
Madhya Pradesh	5	13
Maharashtra	8	3
Odisha	9	12
Punjab	13	5
Rajasthan	6	11
Tamil Nadu	7	6
Uttar Pradesh	1	14
West Bengal	4	10

Source: *State Finances: A Study of Budgets*, RBI and mospi.gov.in.

Table 7.6: Share of Central taxes among 15 major States, 2010-11 to 2014-15

State	Central taxes share rank	Per capita income rank
Andhra Pradesh	5	9
Bihar	2	15
Goa	15	1
Gujarat	11	5
Haryana	14	2
Karnataka	10	8
Kerala	12	6
Madhya Pradesh	4	13
Maharashtra	7	3
Odisha	9	12
Punjab	13	7
Rajasthan	6	11
Tamil Nadu	8	4
Uttar Pradesh	1	14
West Bengal	3	10

Source: *State Finances: A Study of Budgets*, RBI and mospi.gov.in.

Table 7.7: Share of Central grants among 15 major States, 2005-06 to 2009-10

State	Central grants share rank	Per capita income rank
Andhra Pradesh + Telangana	3	9
Bihar	4	15
Goa	15	1
Gujarat	11	4
Haryana	12	2
Karnataka	6	8
Kerala	13	7
Madhya Pradesh	7	13
Maharashtra	2	3
Odisha	10	12
Punjab	14	5
Rajasthan	9	11
Tamil Nadu	8	6
Uttar Pradesh	1	14
West Bengal	5	10

Source: *State Finances: A Study of Budgets*, RBI and mospi.gov.in.

income[3] ones based on per capita incomes, it is seen that the share of the middle-income States in taxes as well as in grants has declined in both the periods 2005-06 to 2009-10 and 2010-11 to 2014-15 (Tables 7.3 and 7.4). The share of high-income States has gone up in grants during the two periods 2005-06 to 2009-10 and 2010-11 to 2015-16 (Tables 7.3 and 7.4). It is relevant to note that during this period, completely untied statutory grants (post-devolution deficit grants recommended by the FCs) constituted only 10-15 per cent of the total and discretionary grants had predominant share (Table 3.6).

THE LIKELY IMPACT OF THE ToR OF THE 15TH FC

The ToR of the 15th FC, which suggests a) examining whether

[3] The States in the categories have remained the same. The middle-income States have been Kerala, Karnataka, Andhra Pradesh (including Telangana), Tamil Nadu and West Bengal. The low-income States have been Rajasthan, Odisha, Madhya Pradesh, Uttar Pradesh and Bihar. The high-income States are Punjab, Goa, Maharashtra, Gujarat and Haryana.

Table 7.8: Share of Central grants among 5 major States, 2010-11 to 2014-15

	Central grants	Per capita income
Andhra Pradesh + Telangana	4	9
Bihar	5	15
Goa	15	1
Gujarat	11	5
Haryana	13	2
Karnataka	9	8
Kerala	12	6
Madhya Pradesh	6	13
Maharashtra	2	3
Odisha	10	12
Punjab	14	7
Rajasthan	7	11
Tamil Nadu	8	4
Uttar Pradesh	1	14
West Bengal	3	10

Source: *State Finances: A Study of Budgets*, RBI and mospi.gov.in.

statutory grants under Article 275 should be there at all; b) reviewing the 'substantial enhancement' in tax devolution consequent to the 14th FC award; and c) bringing back discretionary grants, would make the devolution of resources far less progressive. In the interests of progressivity in devolution of resources, tied grants should be reduced and tax devolution and flexible grants should be made the major components. The ToR of the 15th FC is a movement away from this direction and would adversely affect the progressivity of devolution of resources to the States. In addition to that, the ToR has proved to be an impediment to the freedom of the FC to balance the interests of the States, which are at different levels of fiscal capacity, especially due to its restrictive mandate on use of the population based on the 2011 census.

CHAPTER 8

CENTRE–STATE RELATIONS AND EMPOWERING LOCAL GOVERNMENTS

To carry our statements in Chapter 1 regarding the significance of the federal structure to its logical conclusion, devolution has to be extended from the federal to the local level. Local Governments (LGs) are closer to the people and can go beyond mere representative democracy towards participatory direct democracy. The third tier's close linkage to the people confers it many advantages like greater congruity between needs and expenditure through proper delineation of peoples priorities, exploitation of local production possibilities through use of suitable cost effective technologies and maintenance of assets. Greater participation of people in planning and implementation would lead to higher utilization of local resources in terms of money, material and manpower. The greater transparency that would result from peoples' participation would lead to more accountability and reduction in corruption.

Strengthening of LGs is essential to tap their full potential to achieve effective and efficient governance especially in delivering minimum needs, public services and reduction of poverty. Apart from transfer of mandated functions and functionaries, adequate funds also have to be devolved to LGs commensurate with their responsibilities as a third tier of governance. States are under an obligation to do so in the light of the 73rd and 74th amendments to the Constitution. However, we must guard against the temptation to divorce the discussion on decentralization to the third tier from Centre–State relations.

This is the first issue that we take up in this chapter in the background of a brief historical narrative of the experiments with local government in the post-Independence period. We shall then move on to the salient features of the 73rd and 74th Constitution amendments and the fiscal arrangements therein. We then turn to the experience since the passage of these historic amendments.

The fact that only the Kerala government celebrated the 25th anniversary of the passage of the amendments through a national seminar and an evocative Thiruvananthapuram Declaration (KILA 2018) is commentary on the present state of affairs with regard to democratic decentralization in India. Salient features of the decentralization process in the State of Kerala and the role of the State government assume importance in this context.

Finally, we shall review the stance of the successive Union FCs towards financing the local governments and the ToR of the 15th FC.

THE FAILED ATTEMPTS AT DECENTRALIZATION TO THE 3RD TIER

Grama swaraj was one of the most important ideals of the national movement and a vital component of the Gandhian vision of free India's Constitution (Shriman Narayanan 1946). However, in the Constitution that was drawn up finally by the Constituent Assembly it was relegated to the Directive Principles of State Policy in Article 40. As a consequence, it was not mandatory to have a third tier below the State government and the subject of LGs was left to the discretion of the State governments. The power to constitute 'local government, that is to say, the constitution of powers of municipal corporations, improvement trusts, district boards, mining settlement authorities and other local authorities for the purpose of self-government or village administration' was included in the State List of the Seventh Schedule of the Constitution.

The reason for this turn was the apprehension of many, including Dr B.R. Ambedkar, about the stranglehold of the upper castes and other vested interests at the local level and the likelihood of elite capture. There was no guarantee that the same would not happen at the State and central levels, but it was assumed that these levels of governments would have greater autonomy from the local elite. The possibility of addressing the danger of elite capture at the local level, through affirmative actions, was not explored. In other words, the creation of a democratic space at the local level that could be used for the mobilization of the oppressed and resistance against oppression was not appreciated. In fact, it has been contended that the bureaucratic machinery at the local level, in the absence of an elected supervisory mechanism, was even more amenable to elite capture (Kaviraj 1988, Bhambri 1993). After the failure of repeated attempts to invigorate the LGs along a trajectory with its ups and downs, it took three decades to overcome the vested interests at the central and State levels and make the third tier an inherent part of the government structure in India.

With the advent of planning, the need for a grassroots level administrative structure to implement rural development programmes was realized. This followed from the most persuasive argument for decentralization that fiscal assignment at the lowest tier of government is the most efficient one in terms of provisioning of public services because of the proximity to the revealed choices and preferences of citizens ('principle of subsidiarity', Oates 1972). There was another reasoning in the economic literature about competition among tiers of government closer to people resulting in citizens 'voting with their feet' by moving to the jurisdictions where local service provisioning is best suited to their choices and preferences (Tiebout 1956). However, these principles can work only if there is an effective institutional design, which was sought to be provided in the Indian context by S.K. Dey's[1] Community Bloc Development Scheme. It created a pool of developmental experts below the district level, though only with limited autonomy in planning and implementation of agricultural and rural development programmes sponsored by the central government.

It did not take long to realize that the new decentralized administrative structure of the five-year plan had to be linked to the democratic process at the local level. The Balwant Rai Mehta Committee Report (1957) suggested a revamping of the archaic local government structure that varied from region to region into a national uniform three tier format, viz. Zilla Parishad (ZP) at the district, Panchayat Samiti at the intermediate level and Grama Panchayat (GP) at the local level respectively. The intermediate level was to be coterminous with the development blocks and was to be constituted through indirect election from panchayats. The report was enthusiastically endorsed by the central government and the then prime minister Pandit Jawaharlal Nehru, giving rise to a new generation of panchayats in independent India. However, once the initial enthusiasm waned, particularly after the death of Prime Minister Nehru in 1964, the panchayati raj system too withered away in most parts of the country. The period 1959-1964, was a phase of ascendancy, the period 1965-1969, a phase of stagnation and the subsequent period a phase of decline as far as panchayati raj in India was concerned.

What went wrong? The necessary legislative modifications were carried out in most of the States to usher in the new era of

[1] S.K. Dey was Union Cabinet Minister for Cooperation and Panchayati Raj in the Jawaharlal Nehru government and the person behind the Community Development Scheme of 1953. He was also a member of the Balwant Rai Mehta Committee (1957) set up to study the impact of the scheme.

panchayats. But, the newly elected LGs formed were extremely weak in functions, functionaries and finance. The bureaucracy controlled the intermediate and district levels. The vertical programmes initiated as part of the five-year plans, particularly the components of the Green Revolution strategy, were departmental and hierarchical in nature, discouraging effective local level participation. It was in this context that the Ashok Mehta Committee, which included very eminent scholars and practitioners of panchayati raj, was appointed in 1977 by the NDC.

The most far reaching and innovative suggestion of the Ashok Mehta Committee Report (1978) was amending the Constitution for making the third tier mandatory. In this proposed structure of the three tier system, the district was to be the first point of decentralization. The intermediate level would be converted into non-statutory executive committees of the Zilla Parishad and provide necessary linkages between development schemes and growth centres. At the grassroots level, there would be Mandal panchayats covering a population of 15,000-20,000. Municipalities were to be represented in Zilla Parishads and smaller municipalities were to be considered for merger with Mandal panchayats. The submission of the report gave rise to a new wave of enthusiasm for decentralization and a second generation of panchayats emerged with the most prominent among them in Karnataka, West Bengal and Jammu & Kashmir. Though constitutional amendments had to wait for a decade and more, these State governments took the initiative to revamp their State laws and systems drawing inspiration from the report. What we emphasize here is that the best initiatives in decentralization came from the States, even if they were not shared by all the States.

The decline of the second generation panchayats, other than in the three States mentioned, was even faster than the first generation ones, winning more advocates for the Ashok Mehta Committee's suggestion for constitutional status to LGs. This could be what persuaded Prime Minister Rajiv Gandhi to initiate the 64th and 65th Constitution amendment bills in 1988. The proposals in these bills contained most of the provisions that would later appear in the 73rd and 74th Constitution amendments in 1993. But, there was an outburst of opposition from many quarters including some of the key proponents of the democratic decentralization in the country like E.M.S. Namboodiripad, the first chief minister of Kerala and one who had unsuccessfully attempted to legislate one of the most comprehensive and radical decentralization initiatives ever during 1957-59. He had earlier famously stated: 'Democracy at the central and State levels but bureaucracy at lower levels. This is the essence of Indian polity as spelt out in the Constitution.'[2] Therefore, no one needs to doubt his commitment to the constitutional change. But, he turned out to the severest critic of the proposed 64th and 65th Constitution amendments.

EMS always discussed decentralization as part of Centre–State relations, as can be clearly seen from his note of dissent to the Ashok Mehta Committee Report. He believed that democratic relations between Centre and States were under constant attack and struggle for democracy from the State level downwards had to be brought within the ambit of the former struggle. EMS had criticized the 64th and 65th amendments for bypassing the States and envisaging direct connection of the Centre and the panchayats (Isaac 1998). Direct funding from New Delhi, elections to be organized by the Central Election Commission, administrative control through district collectors, and power of the Governor to dissolve LGs were some of the major points of criticism that were

[2] Note of Dissent to the Ashok Mehta Committee Report (1978), panchayati.gov.in. It is relevant here that decentralization has to be democratic and should facilitate the combination of and cooperation between the official machinery of administration and the non-official leadership and control through the mechanism of LGs (Meenakshisundaram 1994).

raised. The Bill, though passed by the Lok Sabha, failed to receive majority support in the Rajya Sabha and lapsed, when the former was dissolved in 1989, prior to fresh elections. It is pertinent that some scholars have remarked that 'the Centre has thrown away an opportunity to develop a consensus on a matter of national concern and its credibility gap is increasing. The decentralization process must begin with Centre shedding its powers to the States, to be followed thereafter from the State governments to the PRIs' (Chandrasekhar 1989). Nevertheless, these criticisms need not detract from the other positive aspects of the draft Bills which by and large were carried forward to the 73rd and 74th Constitution amendments in 1993.

THE 73RD AND 74TH CONSTITUTION AMENDMENTS: AN OVERVIEW

The 73rd and 74th Constitution amendments were landmarks in the democratic decentralization process in the India. Many of the objections which provoked even the ardent advocates of empowering the LGs to oppose the 64th and 65th Constitution amendment bills, were addressed and resolved by a more pragmatic and least common denominator approach by the then minority government at the Centre headed by Prime Minister Narasimha Rao.

The 73rd and 74th amendment bills provided for formation of panchayats and nagarpalikas (municipalities and corporations) respectively. This segregation of the rural and urban areas at the district level is a major departure from the concept of Zilla Parishads in the Ashok Mehta Committee Report based draft Bill of 1978. Exclusion of nagarpalikas from the ambit of district panchayats precluded the possibility of having an integrated district level government. The district government was the key feature of the EMS government's aborted Bill of 1957, the District Council Act of Kerala, 1979, and the perspective put forward by Ramachandran (1988) on how to implement the District Councils in Kerala. In fact, the first elections to the District Councils were completed in 1990 and the newly elected District Councils were in operation during 1990-91, when they were dissolved by the United Democratic Front (UDF) government, which came to power in 1991. After the passage of the 73rd and 74th Constitution amendments. District panchayats sans the urban areas came into being as part of the three tier structure.

The amendments also introduced uniformity into the three tier system with direct elections at all the levels throughout the country (Articles 243B and 243Q). The most striking feature of the amendments was that five-year elections to LGs were made mandatory (Articles 243E and 243U). If any LGs are dissolved, elections are to be held within a period of six months. The bane of the local government system in India until these constitutional amendments had been the non-conduct of regular elections. Even in a politically sensitive State like Kerala, elections to LGs were not conducted for a period of 18 years at a stretch from the mid-1960s. This had been the most important of factors responsible for the erosion of the credibility of the LGs.

Yet another major change was the constitutional provision for financially empowering the local governments by providing for formation of State FCs which are mandated to secure sound finance of the panchayats by apportioning State revenues between the States and the LGs and assigning revenue sources for appropriation by them (Articles 243I and 243Y). State FCs are also to recommend grants-in-aid to local bodies from the Consolidated Fund of the States. Further, Clauses (3)(bb) and (c) were inserted in Article 280 to mandate the Union FCs to make recommendations for augmenting the Consolidated Funds of the States to fiscally empower LGs. As we shall be discussing at fair length, later in this chapter, grants by the Union FCs have become an important source of untied funds for LGs, even though there is need for change in their approach. In contrast, the performance of State FCs have been lackadaisical in a majority of the States, with their recommendations being very timid and flouted more often than not by the State governments.

The Eleventh and Twelfth Schedules added to the Constitution through these amendments enumerated a list of subjects that the States may transfer to the LGs. It is an enabling list and it is up to the State governments through their Acts to determine the exact subjects to be transferred. Most of the State governments have mechanically transported the entire items in the list into their Acts. Therefore, we have a situation of overlapping functions of States and LGs, many of which are also within the ambit of the Concurrent List with the Centre. What should really have been done was detailed activity mapping so that each function could have been split into a number of activities and those activities which are best undertaken by the local level listed separately. The Mani Shankar Aiyar Committee Report (GoI 2013a) argued that activity mapping is the most fundamental and primary step to be undertaken for proper devolution of functions.

It was through the constitutional amendments with respect to LGs that planning makes entry into our Constitution (Article 243G). The Central Planning Commission had been formed on the basis of an executive order in 1951. On the other hand, the amendment provided for 'preparation of plans for economic development and social justice' as a function of the LGs. Article 243W(b) also provides for district planning committees with the representation of rural and urban local governments and also nominated experts to consolidate the plans from below and draw up district-level perspective plans. In a sense, the District Planning Committee (DPC) is an integrated forum for the entire district. Ironically, just as the DPCs had started to function, the central government abolished the Planning Commission and the planning process in India. But it would require a constitutional amendment to do away with the DPC and the bottom up planning process.

The constitutional amendments also take care of the Fifth Schedule areas by incorporating the provision of the Panchayats (Extension to Scheduled Areas) Act (PESA), 1996, with the intention of safeguarding and promoting the interests of the ST population of these areas.

Reservation for women in Parliament and the legislatures is still a contentious issue, whereas the 73rd and 74th Constitution amendments settled this in so far as LGs are concerned, a quarter century back. One-third of the seats in local governments has been reserved for women (Articles 243D and 243T). Of the 32 lakh elected representatives, 12 lakh are women, i.e. nearly 38 per cent, which is much more than the minimum requirement. Some States like Kerala have increased the representation of women to 50 per cent. There is reservation for women among office bearers also, so that 86,000 women elected representatives are office bearers in LGs. There is also reservation for scheduled castes and scheduled tribes in proportion to their share of population at every level of the panchayati raj system and in urban municipalities. Their numbers are generally marginally in excess of the minimum requirement and in the case of SC/ST women's representation, it is well above the stipulated minimum.

Finally, the popular assembly of people in every locality, the Grama Sabha, has been enshrined in the Constitution (Article 243(b)). In most States, Grama Sabha means the voters' assembly of every hamlet. But in States like Kerala the Grama Sabha is much larger reflecting the large size of its Grama panchayats. Voters in a ward have been defined to constitute the Grama Sabha in Kerala. The functions of the Grama Sabha varies from State to State, but they are mostly advisory in nature. Grama Sabhas constitute forums for direct democracy and in a sense go beyond the normal representative nature of our democratic system.

A REVIEW OF THE EXPERIENCE OF THE LAST QUARTER CENTURY

The constitutional amendments brought about far reaching changes in the federal structure of the country, most of which have been elaborated above, such as, the creation of 2.5 lakh LGs of a uniform pattern throughout the nation to which 32 lakh representatives are elected at regular five-year intervals, with affirmative reservation for women and SCs/STs. According to the 20th Anniversary Report of the Expert Committee on Leveraging Panchayats for Efficient Delivery of Public Goods and Services, 'This is an achievement in political empowerment that, in scale and numbers, is without precedent in history or parallel in the world. Yet, this historic achievement has made little impression on political circles, media perceptions, society as a whole, or even on the rural economy' (GoI 2013a, p. 35).

The report further observed that 'the implementation of the operative core of Part IX relating to devolution of the 3 Fs – functions, finances and functionaries – has been far from in accord with the letter and spirit of the Constitution Amendments'. According to the report, the local governments in India are still a shadow of 'Institutions of self-government' envisaged in the Constitution.

These observations should be viewed against the background that they were made eight years after the Planning Commission (in 2006) had regretted that 'though more than 14 years have gone since constitutional mandate was brought into effect, there has been little progress except in very few states'.

It is quite relevant here to cite the views of Oommen (2018), that

> the roles and responsibilities of local governments remain ill-defined

> despite activity mapping in several States. States control funds, functions and functionaries, making autonomous governance almost impossible. Most States continue to create parallel bodies (often fiefdoms of ministers and senior bureaucrats) that make inroads into the functional domain of local governments. For example, Haryana has created a Rural Development Agency, presided over by the Chief Minister, to enter into the functional domain of panchayats. Legislative approval of these parallel bodies legitimises the process of weakening decentralised democracy. Increasing allocations to Members of Parliament Local Area Development Scheme, or MPLADS, which started in 1993, and their State-level counterparts, known as the MLALADS, hastened the process of euthanasia. There is no mandate to create a DPC tasked to draft a district development plan that takes into account spatial planning, environmental conservation, rural–urban integration, etc. In States like Gujarat, the DPC has not been constituted. A potential instrument to reduce growing regional imbalances is left to rot. [. . .]
>
> Even after 25 years, local government expenditure as a percentage of total public sector expenditure comprising Union, State and local governments is only around 7% as compared to 24% in Europe, 27% in North America and 55% in Denmark. The own source revenue of local governments as a share of total public sector own source revenue is only a little over 2% and if disaggregated, the Panchayat share is a negligible 0.3% (several States like Rajasthan, Punjab and Haryana have abolished property taxes and others do not collect taxes). This speaks of the fiscal weakness of village panchayats.

What is the reason for the above lack of appreciation and tardy progress in democratic decentralization? To unravel this mystery, we have to move from the formal quantitative numbers about the LGs and their representatives, (which no doubt is a worthy achievement in itself), to substantial issues related to the level of devolution of functions, functionaries and funds and the resultant outcomes in governance and development. A simple method would be to examine the devolution indices[3] that have been constructed by specialized institutions for the Ministry of Panchayati Raj from 2005-06. Though the primary aim of this exercise has been to identify the top ranking States in devolution, we may use it to analyse the level of devolution and the range of difference between the States.

The latest study undertaken by Tata Institute of Social Sciences (TISS) for the Ministry of Panchayati Raj (2016) looks at three dimensions, viz. a) operational core of decentralization comprising transfer of functions, functionaries and funds and the extent of autonomy enjoyed by the PRIs; b) achievements in developing support systems for devolution covering capacity building, operationalizing constitutional mechanisms and nurturing systems for accountability and transparency; and c) an incremental index which reflects the progress made during the period 2012-15 in the areas of transfer of functions, funds and functionaries. As already stated, the results of this analysis reveal more than what only the aggregates reveal. They evaluate the pioneers and recent achievers to get a holistic picture.

In the operational core of decentralization ranking Kerala, Tamil Nadu, Maharashtra and Karnataka rank high. In support systems for devolution Kerala retains the top position with Maharashtra in the second position, followed by Karnataka and with Haryana as the number four in the group. In the Incremental index, Andhra Pradesh, Sikkim and Odisha were top performers. It is noteworthy that the States of Kerala and Karnataka, which had a shared history of initiatives in decentralization efforts, even prior to the 73rd

[3] For a critical assessment of the devolution index, see Oommen (2009). The declaration made in the conference held in Thiruvananthapuram to mark the Silver jubilee of the 73rd and 74th Constitution amendments also highlights the need for revising the devolution index (KILA 2018).

and 74th Constitution amendments, have done well in indices of operational core and support systems for decentralization. It is equally disturbing that the States of Uttar Pradesh and Bihar rank low in improvement also, which implies that transition to grassroots level democracy is eluding India's two most populous States.

On the whole, there is a sclerosis in the decentralization process. Only in Kerala is progress visible. Karnataka[4] and West Bengal have seen slippage and in most of the States incremental improvement is minimal. Devolution from the States' Consolidated Funds has been lagging far behind the devolution from the Union's Consolidated Fund. There has also been emergence of parallel agencies, like different development authorities and vertical programmes, which have made inroads into the domain of the LGs.

Yet another major impediment for substantial progress in decentralization to LGs is the lack of any initiative to restructure Centre–State relations in India. The central inroads into the States' expenditure domain are increasing through CSS. In CSS, there is no scope for any flexibility to take account of region specific or location specific factors. In fact, there should be tax devolution and unconditional grants, enabling the States to carry out social and economic sector programmes with the empowered participation of local governments. This would be the true translation of the subsidiarity principle into reality. On the contrary, the delivery of substantial resources through CSS makes the LGs and the States mere agencies rather than equal partners in a federal set up in which they can formulate and implement policies. Nevertheless, it must be said that the close association of MGNREGA with LGs has formally persisted. The reason lies in the rights-based legislation passed by the Parliament, where the scheme is visualized to be implemented through the LGs.

[4] Slippage is from the rank in the devolution index during 2012-13 to that in 2015-16. For a comparative view, see reports prepared for the Ministry of Panchayati Raj by IIPA (2013) and by TISS (2016).

A major obstacle for the vast differences in the decentralization experience across the States is the varying degree of political will. One crucial determinant which builds the political will in the States is the awareness and empowerment enabled by the presence of mass political and social organizations. This builds sustained pressure from below on the State government to decentralize functions, functionaries and funds. The experience of Kerala, which has implemented decentralization to LGs on a mission mode, is a classic example of the above proposition. The regional diversity in performance of decentralization needs to be studied with the purpose of comparing States, so to understand the socio-political factors impeding the implementation of the historic democratic constitutional initiative of decentralization. An in depth analysis of this is beyond the province of this book.

PEOPLE'S PLAN CAMPAIGN AND KERALA'S LOCAL GOVERNMENTS

After repeated and abortive attempts to devolve substantial powers to the local governments, primarily due to lack of political will within the ruling political coalitions, in 1996-2001, the Left Democratic Front (LDF) government adopted an innovative strategy of social mobilization for implementation of democratic decentralization. It was declared that 40 per cent of the plan funds would be devolved to local governments. It meant an increase in the funds devolution from an average of Rs 2 lakh per Grama Panchayat to Rs 75 lakh. But, before this money could be claimed, a comprehensive plan for utilizing the grants had to be prepared. A procedure was laid down for drawing up the plan so that no one was excluded, transparency was assured and objective, scientific deliberation went into the decision making. This planning process involved the participation of lakhs of people in Grama Sabhas, tens of thousands in development seminars, thousands in projectization and drawing up the plan. Thus the technical process of planning was converted into an instrument for social mobilization. That rallied people around the LGs, empowered them and generated pressure from below on the State government for carrying out the necessary devolution.

As stated above, Kerala adopted a Big Bang approach to decentralization by devolving substantial functions and funds along with functionaries to LGs. Though there were some reversals due to transfer of responsibilities preceding capacity building and putting proper systems in place, undoubtedly Kerala has been the forerunner of decentralization in the country. The methodology and approach adopted by Kerala has tremendous scope for replicability in other States with regard to transfer of functions, functionaries and funds to the LGs.

As far as devolution of functions in Kerala is concerned, there is a clear mapping of functions and responsibilities among various tiers of LG and a rational division of functions between the States and the LGs. This is in stark contrast to the national scenario as observed by the 20th Anniversary Report. In the Kerala scheme of things, human development, poverty reduction, local economic development and provision of minimum needs including housing are in the functional realm of LGs. The functions of pre-primary, primary and secondary education, primary and secondary health, basic technical education, nutrition security, social security other than welfare boards, have been devolved fully and those of women and child development, and roads other than major district roads, substantially.

Functionaries have been transferred to LGs with full control over assigning of work, supervision of execution, review of performance and imposition of minor penalties wherever warranted, even while the State government is the staff-creating and cadre-controlling authority. Independent bodies like an Ombudsman and Appellate Tribunal have been formed to ensure accountability and reduce the executive controls of State government.

In the realm of funds, LGs had own tax revenue sources like property tax and profession tax even before the 73rd and 74th Constitution amendments. The State government devolves funds to the LGs under Development, Maintenance and General Purpose funds. The funds transferred under these are substantially untied. It should also be noted that salaries of the transferred functionaries like teachers, doctors, engineers are paid directly by the State government and LGs do not have the obligation of meeting these from the transferred resources. There is transparency in devolution which is recorded separately in an LG budget document by the State government. The flow of funds are predictable based on SFC recommendations and also a fixed share of plan allocation. The periodicity of fund devolution is also consistent.

Till the formation of District Councils in 1990s, Kerala was backward when compared to other States in devolution, despite ideal initial conditions such as high literacy, declining influence of caste and land reforms. The People's Plan Campaign catapulted the State to the front rank, a position it has held consistently till now. Here is the example of a State which has gone beyond the constitutional mandate to empower the LGs and realize the potential of true federal decentralization. Even if one takes the example of any other State, there would definitely be a number of LCs which have done exemplarily well, like those of Kerala. It shows there does exist a democratic space created by the constitutional amendments, which under favourable circumstances can create desirable outcomes. The challenge before the Union FCs and the central government is how to encourage and scale up these positive tendencies. Unfortunately, the BJP government has nothing to its credit in the furtherance of democratic decentralization.

TREATMENT OF LOCAL GOVERNMENTS BY UNION FCs

As already mentioned, consequent to the 73rd and 74th Constitution amendments, Article 280 of the Constitution was also amended by inserting Clause (3)(bb) and (c) which read:

> It shall be the duty of the Commission to make recommendations to the President as to . . . the measures needed to augment the Consolidated Fund of a State to supplement the resources of the Panchayats in the State on the basis of the recommendations made by the Finance Commission of the State . . . [and] the measures needed to augment the Consolidated Fund of a State to supplement the resources of the Municipalities in the State on the basis of the recommendations made by the Finance Commission of the State. . . .

These amendments enabled the Union FCs to devolve grants to the States for fiscally empowering the LGs based on appropriate criteria framed by them. The 10th FC started this though the task was not part of its ToR. The Union FCs since the 11th have been doing this as part of the mandate given in their ToRs. Let us briefly examine the criteria which were the basis of grants for LGs by the 11th to 14th FCs.

AWARDS BY 11TH TO 14TH FCs: A BRIEF OVERVIEW

As already stated, the FCs have been recommending grants to LGs in accordance with the provisions of Article 280(3)(bb) and (c). The quantum of grants recommended by the10th to 14th FCs and the criteria which formed its basis are presented in Tables 8.1 and 8.2 respectively.

The 10th FC devolved Rs 100 per capita for the rural population based on 1971 census and laid down the condition that it should not

Table 8.1: Amount of grants to LGs, 10th to 14th FCs (Rs crore)

Finance Commissions		All States	
		Rural	Urban
Tenth FC		4,380	100
Eleventh FC		8,000	2,000
Twelfth FC		20,000	5,000
Thirteenth FC	Basic Service Grant	39,712	13,971
	Performance Grant	17,471	5,009
Fourteenth FC	Basic Service Grant	18,026	69,715
	Performance Grant	20,029	17,428

Source: Reports of the 10th to 14th Finance Commissions.

Table 8.2: Criteria for grants to LSGs, 10th to 14th FCs (%)

Criteria	10th FC	11th FC	12th FC	13th FC		14thFC
				PRI	ULB	
Index of decentralization		20	10			
Distance from highest per capita income		20	20			
Revenue effort w.r.t. own revenue		5	10			
Revenue effort w.r.t. primary sector GSDP (excluding mining and quarrying)		5	10			
Geographical area		10	10	10	10	10
Population	100					
(1971)	40					
(1991)	40					
(2001)	50	50	90			
(2011)						
Index of devolution				15	15	
Distance from highest per-capita sectoral income				10	20	
SC/ST population				10	-	
FC LG grant utilization				5	5	

Source: Reports of the 10th to 14th Finance Commissions.

be used for payment of salaries and wages. The 11th FC stipulated that the grants had to be used for maintaining core service and should not be used for payment of salaries and wages. The 12th FC stated that the grants are to be used for improving service delivery, creation of database on local finances and maintenance of accounts through the use of modern technology and management systems. The 12th FC, while enlarging the grants to Rs 25,000 crore, tended to limit the fiscal needs of the LGs to traditional civic functions of water supply and sanitation. The 13th and 14th FCs bifurcated the grants into basic and performance-based ones, making the former unconditional, while the latter carried several conditions. The conditions also varied between those for the PRIs and Urban LGs. The 13th FC had further stipulated furnishing of utilization certificates and the maintenance of accounts of local bodies as a condition for the award of performance grants. The 14th FC did away with the requirement of furnishing utilization certificates, but made audited accounts of the two years prior to the current financial year as a condition for performance grants. The ratio in which the basic and performance grants were apportioned was 90:10 for PRIs and 80:20 for urban LGs.

Non-utilization of funds has been a major problem with the LGs. To improve the utilization of funds the 14th FC has recommended that grants should be devolved to the grama panchayats and municipalities, without any time gap by the States.

The FCs have also made recommendations for increasing the efficiency of tax collection by the LGs, periodic revisions in taxes, introduction of new revenue sources such as service charges from State and Union governments for civic services and also matching grants from the State governments.

However, the general approach of the Union FCs regarding the impact of fund devolution to LGs on State finances has been a continuation of the one laid down by the 10th FC, which held that a) it was fiscally neutral and does not result in any extra fiscal burden on the States; and b) there is no need to transfer resources from the Centre as a consequence of decentralization. This view fails to appreciate the enlarged role of the LGs in social and economic development as visualized in the 73rd and 74th

Constitution amendments, besides the traditional civic functions. It is not mere transfer of spending, which is to be undertaken by the State governments in the new scenario after the constitutional amendments. Effective decentralization demands that hitherto neglected areas would have to be identified and measures taken for their upliftment and this would involve substantial additional spending.

Decentralization in the true sense is not replicating what was done till now by the State governments through the LGs in a mechanical manner. It requires an entirely different approach and a wider scope of intervention for social welfare and enhanced capacities, as one can discern from the spirit of the 73rd and 74th Constitution amendments. The lack of appreciation of this has resulted in underestimating the fiscal needs of the States arising from decentralization to LGs. This is the primary reason for commitments consequent to the enlarged role of LGs after the 73rd and 74th Constitution amendments not getting reflected in the recommendations of the Union FCs.

The devolution of functionaries, functions and funds to the LGs is used to rank the States for their decentralization efforts, but the 14th FC dumped this criterion for recommending grants to States for passing on to LGs. It is beyond logic and reason not to include this as a criterion in recommending grants under Article 280(3)(bb) and (c).

It needs to be appreciated that this incentive criterion is not comparable to those used for other specific performance-based grants which are being sought to be put before the FCs, especially the 15th FC. States which devolve substantial funds to LGs get hit by non-adherence to revenue deficit targets as well. The double jeopardy caused by ignoring the devolution of funds by the States to the LGs as a criterion by the Union FCs, while recommending grants to States to fiscally empower the LGs is discriminatory and illogical. It is the anti-federal performance grants, which we have discussed in detail in Chapter 5, that should be eliminated. The devolution to LGs which is a prime constitutional obligation for the States should not be ignored by the Union FCs as a criterion, while considering augmenting Consolidated Funds of the States in accordance with the provisions of Article 280(3)(bb) and (c) of the Constitution.

CHAPTER 9

THE WAY AHEAD: TOWARDS A FEDERAL DEMOCRATIC POLITY

In a succinct remark, while considering the case of *State of Rajasthan vs Union of India* (1977 AIR 1361) in which the dismissal of the State government under Article 356 was challenged, the Supreme Court observed that

> If then our Constitution creates a Central Government which is, 'amphibian', in the sense that it can move either on the federal or unitary plane, according to the needs of the situation and circumstances of a case, the question which we are driven back to consider is whether an assessment of the 'situation' in which the Union Government should move either on the federal or unitary plane are matters for the Union Government itself or for this Court to consider and determine.

This observation makes it abundantly clear that though there is a substantial tilt in favour of the Union in the constitutional scheme of balance of powers, specific acts of the Centre can make a huge difference in the political and fiscal realms. It largely depends on the political attitude of the Centre, whether to resort to the emergency provisions only when dire necessity arises and in accordance with the spirit of the those provisions visualized by the founding fathers of the Constitution or to use them taking refuge under the letter of those provisions rather than their spirit. Past and the contemporary experience evidence the latter. The overuse of Article 356, has warranted judicial intervention more than once, the latest one in the chain of landmark decisions of the Supreme Court is in the case of *Government of NCT of Delhi vs Union of India & Another*, in which the aid and advice of the council of ministers was held to be binding on the Lieutenant Governor except under exceptional circumstances. The necessity of repeated judicial interventions reveals that the federal spirit is not being accorded the pride of place it deserves by successive central governments, despite it being part of the basic structure of the Constitution.

In the fiscal realm also, counter-federal tendencies have been dominant. Under the constitutional scheme of things, buoyant sources of revenue are with the Centre and larger expenditure obligations, especially in the social sector are with the States. The States which collect an average of 38 per cent of total taxes incur 60 per cent of the total expenditure. This vertical imbalance is sought to be corrected through the constitutional mechanism of the FCs.

This constitutional scheme would be defeated in its spirit if the central government through the one-sided ToR tries to undermine the role of the FCs. Untied resource flow from the Centre is more desirable for a robust federal framework rather than tied and conditional grants as the latter restricts the spending freedom of States in subjects enumerated in the State List of the Seventh Schedule of the Constitution. This is against the grain of a healthy federal system. In the Indian context, flexible and untied resource flows have declined during the 12th and 13th FC periods but the 14th FC has reversed this trend (Table 3.6). But the ToR of the 15th FC signals a turnaround.

Besides, the untied flow of resources, 90 per cent of which is tax devolution, is getting shrunk through actions of the central government, at a time when there is wide perception that the devolution of taxes has been 'substantially' enhanced to 42 per cent by the 14th FC when compared to 32 per cent in the 13th FC award. This is being done in more than one way, viz. resorting to increasing levy of surcharges and cesses, and non-transparency in computation of net proceeds. The substantial losses arising from these actions which shrink the divisible pool of taxes shareable with the States have been discussed in detail in Chapter 3. Apart from reduced resource transfer, these actions go against the constitutional spirit of fiscal federalism.

It is over and above this that the fiscal space of the States are being sought to be constrained further through uniform FRBM targets without considering State-wise specificities and by apportioning GST rates without even considering the principle of revenue neutrality, which was put forth in committees of the Government of India.

It is in this background that the ToR of the 15th FC have been notified with several discriminatory items, which if implemented, can result in substantial weakening of the fragile architecture of fiscal federalism. These have been discussed elaborately in Chapter 5 and are not repeated here. However, not considering the States as equal partners in national priorities and attempting to dub welfare schemes of the States as 'populist' in order to control them is against the basic constitutional scheme and is not in accordance with the Directive Principles of State Policy. These items should not have found a place in the ToR of the 15th FC.

It needs emphasis that the constitutional tilt in powers needs to be balanced by political acts of the Union so that the federal structure becomes robust. Actions to the contrary only increase the imbalances. In other words, the federal foundation is becoming more and more fragile on the fiscal side. The political framework has enabled the Union to make intrusions into the State subjects, through CSS. The States have to incur a part of their cost of implementation without any say in their formulation. In short, cooperative federalism in which the different jurisdictions have to be equal partners has been consciously undermined.

In the context of worsening vertical imbalances, the constitutional mandate of the FC in acting to balance diverse interests of the various States has been stymied and the degrees of freedom restricted through items in the ToR of the 15th FC, which mandates use of population based on the 2011 census while making recommendations. This would exacerbate the inter-State disparities in fiscal devolution and would adversely affect the States which have earnestly implemented the National Population Policy, 1977, by substantially lowering their *inter se* share in tax devolution. This would also be to the detriment of cooperative federalism. When post-tax devolution specific needs of States can be addressed through grants under Article 275, item 5 of the ToR mandates the 15th FC to examine whether these grants should be there at all. The accommodating space for States at vastly different levels of fiscal capacity is being consciously ignored and the flexibility of the FC to delicately balance the interests of all States is being restrained.

The persistence and exacerbation of the skewness in fiscal relations between the Centre and the States also impede any meaningful decentralization to the LGs as discussed at length in Chapter 8.

These acts cumulatively undermine the foundations of fiscal federalism in our country. For building a strong federal and democratic polity the Centre, States and the LGs should be equal stakeholders in the drive to achieve national goals. The Centre–State relations should become more consultative. While constitutional provisions like Article 356, which are unitary in nature are the much used ones, the provisions providing for consultative mechanisms like Article 263 on Inter-State Councils have remained dormant. This is a clear reflection of the lack of will to strengthen the federal foundations. The doing away with the planning process at the national level has deprived the States of a forum like the National Development Council, where State political executives could at least voice their opinion.

If we are to move ahead to be a meaningful federal and democratic polity, the Centre which is endowed with asymmetric political and fiscal powers has to take initiative to reverse this trend. The ToR of the FCs should be subject to formal consultations with the States, which in turn should consult LGs before forming an opinion on this.

Democratically elected State governments and LGs should not be viewed as lower tiers in a pyramidal hierarchy by the Centre. They are in fact, jurisdictions where different policies and programmes have been tried and tested before they became national schemes. Each jurisdiction is an equal stakeholder and is a laboratory where political and economic experiments are carried on. For these to be successful, centralizing tendencies have to remain subdued and subordinated to principles of federalism.

In this context, it is worth mentioning that in pursing their development path some States have become role models for national policies. Kerala has attracted worldwide attention, as the State had attained Human Development Indicators (HDIs) comparable to that of advanced counties, but at much lower levels of per capita income. This was made possible by state intervention in the education and health sectors, along with non-state initiatives. The State also witnessed substantial social pressure through agitations and articulation of opinions in the public domain in favour of universalization of the provision of social services. Presently, Kerala requires resources to bridge the gaps in its development path. The discernible gaps are deficiency in physical capital infrastructure and addressing issues of sections of the population who continue to remain marginalized. The present squeeze on resources and constraints on spending capacity are impeding the State's ability to address these issues, despite a very strong political will and social consciousness. The capping of deficits through legislations laying down stringent deficit targets and central transfers becoming more and more conditional are disabling factors against States formulating their own development programmes. In the current context, replicating the internationally appreciated Kerala-type development experience would be an extremely challenging task. It is strongly felt that uniform targets in the name of fiscal discipline are in fact making federalism lose its essence by preventing jurisdictions from developing paths worth emulation by others. Fiscal discipline should be an enabling factor for development and not an impediment to fiscal empowerment. It is in this context, that caution is advocated and the need to take into account specific contexts instead of prescribing across the board targets is emphasized.

The aspect that is sought to be highlighted here at the cost of reiteration is that the Centre should take the initiative in making the system more federal and consultative. If the contrary process of fiscally disempowering the States in the name of fiscal consolidation continues, not only would the federal foundations be damaged, but also the capacity for social sector intervention of the state as a whole would be circumscribed. This would not augur well for a constitutional set up in which Directive Principles have imposed an obligation to create a welfare state. Past and present aberrations need substantial correction to move on to the path of a more federal and democratic polity.

REFERENCES

Agarwal, Shriman Narayan. 1946. *Gandhian Constitution for Free India*. Allahabad: Kitabistan.

Austin, Granville. 1966. *The Indian Constitution: Cornerstone of a Nation*. Delhi: Oxford University Press.

Bagchi, Amaresh, J.L. Bajaj and William A. Byrd (eds). 1992. *State Finances in India*. New Delhi: Vikas Publishing House.

Bardhan, Pranab. 1984. *Political Economy of Development in India*. Oxford and New York: Basil Blackwell.

Bhambri, C.P. 1993. 'Conflicts and Contradictions within the Indian State'. *Social Scientist*, No. 5/6, May-June.

Bharadwaj, Krishna. 1982. 'Regional Differentiation in India'. *Economic and Political Weekly*, Vol. 17, No. 14-15-16, April 17.

Byres, Terrence J. (ed.). 1998. *The Indian Economy: Major Debates Since Independence*. Delhi: Oxford University Press.

Chandra, Bipin, Mridula Mukherjee and Aditya Mukherjee. 2008. *India since Independence*. New Delhi: Penguin Books.

Chandrasekhar, C.P., and Jayati Ghosh. 2000. *The Market that Failed: Neoliberal Economic Reforms in India*. New Delhi: LeftWord Books.

———. 2001. 'Fiscal Responsibility: To Whom?'. Available at www.macroscan.com.

———. 2005a. 'The Crisis of State Government Debt'. Available at www.macroscan.com.

———. 2005b. 'The Death of Fiscal Federalism'. Available at www.macroscan.com.

Chakraborty, Pinaki, and Lekha Chakraborty. 2018. 'Time to Recast

Union Government Expenditure Needs, New FRBM Framework'. *Economic and Political Weekly*, Vol. 53, No. 9, March 3.

Chakravarthy, Sukhamoy. 1987. *Development Planning: The Indian Experience*. Oxford: Clarendon Press.

Choudhury, Mita. 2018. 'The National Health Protection Scheme in the Union Budget 2018: Is it in the Right Direction?'. nipfp.org.in, February 3.

Chaudhuri, Saumitra. 2000. 'State Government Finances'. *Money and Finance*, ICRA Bulletin, Vol. 2, No. 1, May-June.

Economic and Political Weekly Research Foundation. 2004. 'Special Statistics-37: Finances of State Governments: Deteriorating Fiscal Management'. *Economic and Political Weekly*, Vol. 39, No. 18, May 1.

Government of India. 1978. Committee on Panchayati Raj Institutions, Chairman, Ashok Mehta.

———. 1987. Commission to Examine and Review the Existing Arrangements between the Union and the States, Chairman, Justice R.S. Sarkaria.

———. 2004. *Report of Task Force on Implementation of the FRBM Act*. Chairman, Dr Vijay Kelkar. New Delhi: Ministry of Finance.

———. 2006. *Towards Faster and More Inclusive Growth: An Approach to the Eleventh Five-Year Plan*. New Delhi: Planning Commission, June.

———. 2010. Commission on Centre–State Relations, Chairman, Justice M.M. Punchhi.

———. 2011. *Report of the Committee on Restructuring of Centrally Sponsored Schemes (CSS)*. New Delhi: Planning Commission, September.

———. 2013a. *Twentieth Anniversary Report of the Expert Committee on Leveraging Panchayats for Efficient Delivery of Public Goods and Services*. Chairman, Mani Shankar Aiyar.

———. 2013b. *Strengthening of Panchayats in India: Comparing Devolution across States. Empirical Assessment, 2012-13*. New Delhi: Ministry of Panchayati Raj and The Indian Institute of Public

Administration (IIPA).

———. 2015a. *Report of the Sub-Group of Chief Ministers on Rationalisation of Centrally Sponsored Schemes*. New Delhi: NITI Aayog, October.

———. 2015b. Committee on Revenue Neutral Rates (RNR) under GST, Chairman, Arvind Subramanian, Chief Economic Advisor.

———. 2016. *Devolution Report 2015-16: Where Local Democracy and Devolution India is heading towards?*. Ministry of Panchayati Raj, and Mumbai: Tata Institute of Social Sciences.

Government of Kerala. 1988. *Report of the Committee on the Measures to be taken for Democratic Decentralisation at the District and Lower Levels*, Chairman, V. Ramachandran. Thiruvananthapuram: Government press.

———. 2001. White Paper on State Finances. Thiruvananthapuram: Finance Department.

———. 2003. Memorandum Presented to the Twelfth Finance Commission. Thiruvananthapuram: Finance Department.

———. 2009. Memorandum Presented to the Twelfth Finance Commission. Thiruvananthapuram: Finance Department.

———. 2018. Memorandum Presented to the Fifteenth Finance Commission. Thiruvananthapuram: Finance Department.

Government of Tamil Nadu. 1971. Centre–State Relations Enquiry Committee, Chairman, Justice P.V. Rajamannar.

Government of West Bengal. 1977. Memorandum on Centre–State Relations.

Gulati, I.S., and K.K. George. 1988. *Essays in Federal Financial Relations*. New Delhi: Oxford & IBH Publishing Company Pvt Ltd.

IMF. 2011. *Government Finance Statistics: Compilation Guide for Developing Countries*. Available at: https://www.imf.org/external/pubs/ft/gfs/manual/compil.pdf.

Kaviraj, Sudipta. 1988. 'A Critique of the Passive Revolution'. *Economic and Political Weekly*, Vol. 23, No. 45-47, November 19.

Kerala Institute of Local Administration (KILA). 2018. 'Silver Jubilee

Declaration'. National Conference on 25 years of Panchayati Raj. Thrissur: KILA, April 25.

Kumar, Dharma. 1999. 'The Fiscal System'. In *Cambridge Economic History of India*, Volume 2, c.1757-c.1970, edited by Dharma Kumar and Tapan Raychaudhuri. Cambridge University Press

Kurian, N.J. 1999. 'State Government Finances: A Survey of Recent Trends'. New Delhi: Committee Attached to the Ministry of Finance, Government of India.

Hajra, Kumudini, Rajeev Jain and Dhirendra Gajbhiye. 2009. *Determinants of Surplus Cash Balances of States in India: A Panel Data Analysis*. Reserve Bank of India, December 15.

Meenakshisundaram, S.S. 1994. *Decentralisation in Developing Countries*. Delhi: Concept Publishing Company.

Mitra, Ashok. 1987. 'Will Growth and Centralised Fiscal Arrangements Do?'. In *Centre-State Budgetary Transfers*, edited by I.S. Gulati. Delhi: Oxford University Press.

Mohan, R., and D. Shyjan. 2010. 'Tax Devolution and Grant Distribution to States in India: Analysis and Roadmap for Alternatives'. Working Paper No. 419, Centre for Development Studies (Thiruvananthapuram).

Namboodiripad, E.M.S. 1968. 'Republican Constitution in the Struggle for Socialism'. R.R. Kale Memorial Lecture, Gokhale Institute of Economics and Politics (Pune).

———. 1973. 'On Intermediate Regimes'. *Economic and Political Weekly*, Vol. 8, No. 48, December 1.

———. 1978. 'Note of Dissent on the Ashok Mehta Committee Report'. Ministry of Panchayati Raj, Government of India.

Noorani, A.G. 2012. 'Treaties and States'. *Frontline*, Vol. 29, No. 2, January 28-February 10.

Oates, Wallace E. 1972. *Fiscal Federalism*. New York: Harcourt Brace Jovanovich.

Oommen, M.A. 2009. 'Limits of a "Devolution Index"'. *Economic and Political Weekly*, Vol. 44, No. 29, July 18.

———. 2018a. 'Local Democracy in Disarray'. *The Hindu*, May 1.

———. 2018b. 'Shifting Towards the Centre'. *Business Line*, October 4.

Pankaj, Ashok. 2017. 'Governor in Indian Federalism–II: Hiatus between Constitutional Intents and Practices'. *Indian Journal of Public Administration*, Vol. 63, No. 1.

Patnaik, Prabhat. 1979. 'Industrial Development in India Since Independence'. *Social Scientist*, Vol. 7, No. 11, June.

———. 2000. 'On Some Common Macroeconomic Fallacies'. *Economic and Political Weekly*, Vol. 35, No. 15, April 8.

———. 2001. 'On Fiscal Deficits and Real Interest Rates'. *Economic and Political Weekly*, Vol. 36, No. 14-15, April 7.

———. 2014. 'End of Planning Commission?'. *Economic and Political Weekly*, Vol. 49, No. 29, July 19.

Raj, K.N. 1973. 'Politics and Economics of "Intermediate Regimes"'. *Economic and Political Weekly*, Vol. 8, No. 27-52, July 7.

Rajaraman, Indira, and N.J. Kurian. 2006. 'Report of the Public Expenditure Review Committee'. Thiruvananthapuram: Finance Department, Government of Kerala.

Ramalingam, N. 2017. 'Apportionment of GST Rates between Centre and the States'. Unpublished Note, Gulati Institute of Finance and Taxation (GIFT) (Thiruvananthapuram).

Rao, M. Govinda, and Rajah Chellaiah. 1991. 'A Survey of Research on Fiscal Federalism in India'. Monograph Series II, National Institute of Public Finance and Policy (New Delhi).

———. 1992. 'A Proposal for State-level Budgetary Reforms'. Working Paper 19, National Institute of Public Finance and Policy (New Delhi).

———. 2002. 'State Finances in India: Issues and Challenges'. *Economic and Political Weekly*, Vol. 37, No. 31, August 3.

———, and R. Kavita Rao. 2005. 'Trends and Issues in Tax Policy and Reforms in India'. *Brookings Papers on Economic Activity*, Vol. 2, No. 1, January. Available at: https://www.brookings.edu>2005_rao.

———. 2015. 'Central Transfers to States in India: Rewarding Performance while Ensuring Equity'. NITI Aayog, Government of India.

———. 2018. 'Mandate and Allocations'. *The Hindu*, April 16.

Reinhart, C.M. and Kenneth Rogoff. 2008. 'This Time is Different: A Panoramic View of Eight Centuries of Financial Crisis'. Working Paper No. 13882, March, National Bureau of Economic Research (Cambridge, MA).

———. 2010. 'Growth in a Time of Debt'. Working Paper No. 15639, January, National Bureau of Economic Research (Cambridge, MA).

Reserve Bank of India. 2005a. *State Finances: A Study of Budgets of 2005-06*. Mumbai: RBI, December.

———. 2005b. *Report on the Advisory Committee on Ways and Means Advances to State Governments*, Chair, M.P. Bezbaruah. Mumbai: RBI, October.

———. 2005c. *Annual Report 2004-05*. Mumbai: RBI, August.

———. 2005d. *Handbook of Statistics on the Indian Economy 2004-05*. Mumbai: RBI, September.

———. 2006. *Annual Report 2005-06*. Mumbai: RBI, September.

———. 2018. *State Finances: A Study of the Budgets, 2018-19*. Mumbai: RBI.

State Planning Board, Kerala. 2006. 'A Background Note on the Approach Paper to the Eleventh Five-Year Plan'. Thiruvananthapuram: Government of Kerala.

Thomas Isaac, T.M. 1998. 'EMS on Economics and Politics of Decentralisation'. *The Marxist*, Vol. 24, No. 01-02, Jan-June.

———, and R. Ramakumar. 2006. 'Why do the States not Spend?'. *Economic and Political Weekly*, Vol. 41, No. 48, December 4.

———, and Pinaki Chakraborty. 2018. 'Inter-governmental Transfers: Disquieting Trends and the Thirteenth Finance Commission'. *Economic and Political Weekly*, Vol. 43, No. 43, October 25.

———. 2018a. 'An Open Letter to Finance Ministers'. *The Hindu*, May 14.

———. 2018b. 'Centre Must Not Micromanage Finance Commission'. *Business Standard*, July 14.

Vithal, B.P.R., and M.L. Sastry. 2001. *Fiscal Federalism in India*. New Delhi: Oxford University Press.

Zeitler, Franz-Christoph. 2005. *What Remains of the Stability and Growth Pact?*. Frankfurt: Deutsche Bundesbank.